"An excellent handbook for the defense of Christian beliefs in today's society. Compiled with historical information and biblical references, this book is easily a teaching tool. Be prepared to feel emboldened in your faith and encouraged in your beliefs."

— Andy Whitt
Member of the Alabama House of Representatives

"I have read Ben Stevenson's book with great interest. I am a Christian who loves The Lord first and have recently served in the Tennessee State Legislature for 8 years. Ben understands the dynamics of a Christian living in a world that is dominated by politics. His insight into history, the Bible, and the opportunities and responsibilities Christian have in relation to politics and the world are important for every Christian to read and consider. I highly recommend "The Political Conscience of the Christian."

— Sheila Butt,
Former member Tennessee House of Representatives

THE POLITICAL CONSCIENCE
OF THE CHRISTIAN

BEN STEVENSON

To current, past, and former students: It has always been my attempt to keep my personal political views outside of the classroom. Sometimes I am successful in that endeavor and other times I am not. I have always tried to do so because I want you to come to your own conclusions.

I want to present a case to you and let you do your own independent thinking in coming to a conclusion. With the publication of this book, you will now have more of an inside look at my political mind and where it is rooted. Some of you will agree, and others won't. I hope that you take the information written here and treat it the same way you would a lecture in my class

I have presented a case, now use your own independent thinking and come to a conclusion.

CONTENTS

INTRODUCTION

How can we mingle religion and politics in our lives? Are we not supposed to keep them separate? As a Christian, not only can we mingle the two, but we must. It is a lack of a biblical worldview, for the most part, that has lead us down the political path on which we currently find ourselves, and it is only through a biblical worldview that we can ever come to find the correct path again. It has long been said that the two things that men shouldn't discuss are government and religion. These two topics are seen as taboo when meshed together in public conversation. Although I agree with the sentiment that no minister should stand before his congregation and direct their vote to a particular candidate or party, a man who considers himself religious should be incapable of participating in politics without his religion playing a factor in his decision-making processes. It was God who ordained civil government, and we would do well to yield to Him as we move about as citizens of this nation.

Religion must not be political in nature, but politics without religion will lead to one of the two far sides of the political spectrum: tyranny or anarchy. The political spectrum has existed since the creation of government, and every American today will find himself somewhere along that spectrum. Unfortunately, so many Christians today define their position as affiliated with a certain political party. This is not only dangerous, but it is ill-advised. How then should we know where we stand? I believe President Harry Truman made it clear enough when he said, "If men and nations would but live by the precepts of the ancient prophets and the teachings of the Sermon on the Mount, problems which now seem so difficult would soon disappear."[1] Simply put, it is through the principles found in scripture that we should make all decisions in life, including those of a political nature. If we separate our religion from politics, then we live two separate lives. We live one life as a Christian and one as an American. This does not only hurt the fabric of our nation but, more importantly, it threatens to condemn our soul.

As Christians, we have been blessed in America with dual citizenship. We are citizens of the greatest nation the world has ever seen. Yet, more importantly, we are citizens of an eternal kingdom that is ruled by the Creator of the entire world. Ephesians 2:19-22 reminds us of this when it says, "Now, therefore, you are no longer strangers and foreigners, but fellow citizens with the saints and members of the household of God, having been built on the foundation of the apostles and prophets, Jesus Christ Himself being the chief cornerstone, in whom the whole building, being fitted together, grows into a holy temple in the Lord, in whom you also are being built together for a dwelling place of God in the Spirit." God has indeed blessed this nation throughout time and history. No nation has risen to power faster or with more prestige than the United States. However, no "nation" has or will be more powerful than the one for which Christ died. Even Abraham, the man who God said He would "make the father of many nations" (Genesis 17:4), understood that it was a city he had not yet seen that would

---

1. The Church's Role in the World 2009.

be most wonderful. "These all died in faith, not having received the promises, but having seen them afar off were assured of them, embraced them and confessed that they were strangers and pilgrims on the earth. For those who say such things declare plainly that they seek a homeland. And truly if they had called to mind that country from which they had come out, they would have had opportunity to return. But now they desire a better, that is, a heavenly country. Therefore God is not ashamed to be called their God, for He has prepared a city for them" (Hebrews 11:13-16).

It is not the goal of this book to endorse any particular political party but only to look at some of the issues at hand. I am not personally registered with either of the two major political parties; however, as a Christian who is a scholar, educator, and active participant in the "American experiment," I do feel that it is necessary to shed light on the Biblical worldview of politics in an ever-changing culture and society. There are, of course, many different topics within the various political platforms. We will not take the time to examine all of these but will instead spend our time on many of the issues that have become contradictory to the Bible.

Throughout these pages, we will examine both the scripture and the words of the men who helped shape our country at its origin. The two most important documents in our society today are the Holy Bible and the American Constitution. One dictates the path of us as citizens, and the other dictates the path of us as men. We must stand firm on the issues at hand and never compromise to the pressures of an ever-conforming society. We can see first-hand the dangers of being pleasing to men if only we look in John 19. Pilate made it clear to the crowd that he found no fault in Christ, yet he gave Him over to them to be crucified. If we fail to stand behind our convictions and compromise in the face of political adversity, then we are no better than Pilate. The pillars and principles that helped to found this great nation have never changed, and they are just as much rooted in Genesis as they are in John Locke. The problem, therefore, does not lie with the principles themselves but with the people who interpret these principles. It is our responsibility as Christian Americans to advocate for a government that engenders the ideas and concepts of a Biblical worldview. It is through this mindset that we can bring back the basic pillars on which our government was founded, and we can be advocates for an America that remains in God's favor. God bless you all, and God bless the United States.

"Be still, and know that I am God; I will be exalted among the nations, I will be exalted in the earth!" (Psalm 46:10).

1

TEAR DOWN THIS WALL

The wall of separation between church and state is a phrase that has been misinterpreted by the courts in this country for many years. Who built the wall? Ultimately the answer to that question is Thomas Jefferson; however, he did not build the wall as it is inferred by our judicial system today. In 1802, President Thomas Jefferson responded to a letter sent to him from the Danbury Baptist Association (DBA). In their letter, the DBA had expressed concern that their simple Baptist association may soon be disbanded. (See Appendix A for letters between Jefferson and DBA).

Jefferson had indeed built a wall, but it was not a wall that contained bricks and mortar. Jefferson had merely stated that as a strict constitutionalist and firm believer in the words of the 1st Amendment neither he nor any other form of federal government would be doing anything to destroy the DBA, and for that matter, no other religious group need feel threatened either.

The Bill of Rights was one of the first things on the agenda for a newly elected Congress. It had been a promise made to those Anti-Federalists who refused to ratify the Constitution without their rights individually listed. It was the "Father of the

Constitution" himself, James Madison, who was the leader in producing the Bill of Rights. He originally purposed 9 articles to be considered as fundamental rights of the people. From there, these articles moved about through the House and the Senate and reached as many as 17 articles before twelve were decided upon. In late September of 1789, both houses of Congress approved of the 12 articles, and they were sent to the states for ratification. On December 15, 1791, Virginia became the 10th of 14 states to ratify ten of the original twelve articles, and the Bill of Rights was added to the Constitution with a two-thirds vote.[1]

For a deeper understanding of the 1st Amendment, it helps to look into some of the original proposals:

- June 8, 1789- James Madison "The civil rights of none shall be abridged on account of religious belief or worship, nor shall any national religion be established, nor shall the full and equal rights of conscience be in any manner, or on any pretext infringed."

- August 15, 1789- House Select Committee "No religion shall be established by law, nor shall the equal rights of conscience be infringed."

- August 15, 1789- Samuel Livermore "Congress shall make no laws touching religion, or infringing the rights of conscience."

- August 20, 1789- Fisher Ames "Congress shall make no law establishing religion, or to prevent the free exercise thereof, or to infringe the rights of conscience."[2]

---

1. Chapter 1 (Barton 1992, 27).
2. Ibid.

It was Ames's proposal that was agreed upon and then sent to the Senate who began to work on the wording themselves:

- September 3, 1789- "Congress shall not make any law infringing the rights of conscience, or establishing any religious sect or society."
- September 3, 1789- "Congress shall make no law establishing any particular denomination of religion in preference to another, or prohibiting the free exercise thereof, nor shall the rights of conscience be infringed."
- September 3, 1789- Congress shall make no law establishing one religious society in preference to others, or to infringe on the rights of conscience."
- September 9, 1789- "Congress shall make no law establishing articles of faith or a mode of worship, or prohibiting the free exercise of religion."[3]

The wording from September 9th was then sent back to a Conference Committee in the House and then returned to the full House and Senate where it was finally approved as they set the final wording that we see today: "Congress shall make no law respecting an establishment of religion, or prohibiting the free exercise thereof."

It is evident from the original wording of this part of the First Amendment that religion was intended to be very much a part of life in the early United States. In fact, many of those in the first Congress were relying on their own state constitutions when determining how the First Amendment was to be worded. Look at this excerpt from the Massachusetts Constitution of 1780:

---

3.   Ibid.

- Part I, Article II: It is the right, as well as the duty, of all men in society, publicly, and at states seasons, to worship the Supreme Being, the Great Creator and Preserver of the Universe. And no subject shall be hurt, molested, or restrained, in his person, liberty, or estate, for worshipping God in the manner and season, most agreeable to the dictates of his own conscience.

- Part I, Article III: And every denomination of Christians demeaning themselves peaceably, and as good subjects of the commonwealth, shall be equally under the protection of the law: And no subordination of any one sect or denomination to another, shall ever be established by law.[4]

The Bill of Rights is ultimately a list of what the federal government cannot infringe upon; therefore, leaving it to the state and local governments. Why then, would states ratify part of a document that limits federal government but also is in contradiction with their own state governments? Simply put, the point of what we now call the "Establishment Clause" and "Free Exercise Clause" of the First Amendment were not to separate religion from the federal government. Had that been the intention, no states would have ratified it simply because of what they had already agreed upon within their respective states. The purpose of the First Amendment was to declare, for certain, that the federal government could not create a national religion or prohibit anyone's right to practice their particular religion. That point seems to be clearly stated in the original text, but somehow over time, many have lost sight of the intent.

President Jefferson did not erect a wall of separation between church and state. He simply reminded those members

---

4.   Ibid., 28.

of the Danbury Baptist Association that, as the chief executive of our federal government, he was not at liberty to abolish the religious liberty that they had as citizens of this nation. History is evident and clear about the purpose and meaning for the First Amendment. No man at the time of our nation's origin, including President Jefferson, intended for the First Amendment to be anything more than what is said.

BUILDING THE WALL IN THE COURTS
ENGEL V. VITALE (1962)

The issue at hand, in this case, was that the Board of Regents for the State of New York authorized this short prayer to be recited at the beginning of each school day: "Almighty God, we acknowledge our dependence upon Thee, and beg Thy blessings upon us, our teachers, and our country."[5] As a current teacher of a public school system, I would love for this prayer to be recited before the school day begins. In fact, I can hardly think of a better way to start each day. Unfortunately, the court did not see it the same way. In a 6-1 decision with two members abstaining, the court ruled, with Justice Hugo Black giving the majority opinion, that neither the prayer's non-denominational character nor its voluntary character saved it from unconstitutionality and that by providing the prayer, New York officially approved religion. The problem with this decision is that nowhere in the Constitution does it deny the state or federal government to approve religion. In fact, from the excerpts we have already read in this chapter, it was not only approved but encouraged at our nation's founding. This is simply one of many examples where members of the United States Supreme Court have erected a wall of separation that simply does not exist. The lone dissenter, in this case, was Justice

---

5. Engel v. Vitale 1962.

Potter Stewart. In his dissenting opinion, he not only lays out the reasons that he feels his colleagues got this case wrong, but he goes back to the truth behind the First Amendment.

"A local school board in New York has provided that those pupils who wish to do so may join in a brief prayer at the beginning of each school day, acknowledging their dependence upon God and asking His blessing upon them and upon their parents, their teachers, and their country. The Court today decides that, in permitting this brief nondenominational prayer, the school board has violated the Constitution of the United States. I think this decision is wrong.

The Court does not hold, nor could it, that New York has interfered with the free exercise of anybody's religion. For the state courts have made clear that those who object to reciting the prayer must be entirely free of any compulsion to do so, including any "embarrassments and pressures." Cf. West Virginia State Board of Education v. Barnette, 319 U. S. 624. But the Court says that, in permitting school children to say this simple prayer, the New York authorities have established "an official religion."

With all respect, I think the Court has misapplied a great constitutional principle. I cannot see how an "official religion" is established by letting those who want to say a prayer say it. On the contrary, I think that to deny the wish of these school children to join in reciting this prayer is to deny them the opportunity of sharing in the spiritual heritage of our Nation.

The Court's historical review of the quarrels over the Book of Common Prayer in England throws no light for me on the issue before us in this case. England had then and has now an established church. Equally unenlightening, I think, is the history of the early establishment and later rejection of an official church in our own

States. For we deal here not with the establishment of a state church, which would, of course, be constitutionally impermissible, but with whether school children who want to begin their day by joining in prayer must be prohibited from doing so. Moreover, I think that the Court's task, in this as in all areas of constitutional adjudication is not responsibly aided by the uncritical invocation of metaphors like the "wall of separation," a phrase nowhere to be found in the Constitution. What is relevant to the issue here is not the history of an established church in sixteenth-century England or in eighteenth-century America, but the history of the religious traditions of our people, reflected in countless practices of the institutions and officials of our government.

At the opening of each day's Session of this Court, we stand, while one of our officials invokes the protection of God. Since the days of John Marshall, our Crier has said, "God save the United States and this Honorable Court." Both the Senate and the House of Representatives open their daily Sessions with prayer. Each of our Presidents, from George Washington to John F. Kennedy, has, upon assuming his Office, asked the protection and help of God.

The Court today says that the state and federal governments are without constitutional power to prescribe any particular form of words to be recited by any group of the American people on any subject touching religion. One of the stanzas of "The Star-Spangled Banner" made our National Anthem by Act of Congress in 1931, contains these verses:

"Blest with victory and peace, may the heav'n rescued land"
"Praise the Pow'r that hath made and preserved us a nation,"

"Then conquer we must, when our cause it is
just."
"And this be our motto 'In God is our Trust.'"

In 1954, Congress added a phrase to the Pledge
of Allegiance to the Flag so that it now contains the
words "one Nation under God, indivisible, with liberty
and justice for all." In 1952, Congress enacted legislation calling upon the President each year to proclaim a
National Day of Prayer. Since 1865, the words "IN GOD
WE TRUST" have been impressed on our coins.

Countless similar examples could be listed, but
there is no need to belabor the obvious. It was all
summed up by this Court just ten years ago in a single
sentence: "We are a religious people whose institutions
presuppose a Supreme Being." Zorach v. Clauson, 343
U. S. 306, 343 U. S. 313.

I do not believe that this Court, or the Congress, or
the President has, by the actions and practices I have
mentioned, established an "official religion" in violation of the Constitution. And I do not believe the State
of New York has done so in this case. What each has
done has been to recognize and to follow the deeply
entrenched and highly cherished spiritual traditions of
our Nation -- traditions which come down to us from
those who almost two hundred years ago avowed their
"firm Reliance on the Protection of divine Providence"
when they proclaimed the freedom and independence
of this brave new world."[6]

Few words have ever painted the intent of the First Amendment more purely than those of Justice Stewart in this case.
He not only references the religious heritage that riddles our

---

6.   Ibid.

history, but he also points out how that same heritage still exists. The fact that Justice Stewart was the only one who shared in this opinion just goes to further show how the courts and many of the people of these United States have left the original intent and principles on which the nation was founded.

On June 12, 1987, President Ronald Reagan made a speech in West Berlin calling out the leader of the Soviet Union, Mikhail Gorbachev, to tear down the Berlin wall which had been the barrier between West and East Berlin since 1961. In his famous closing statement, President Reagan said, "Mr. Gorbachev, tear down this wall!" I believe it is time that we, as Christians, tear down the wall that has been erected between church and state. It is not a wall that was ever meant to exist as a means of removing religion from our government, and it is not a wall that can exist if we wish to be One Nation under God.

2

THE RIGHT PEOPLE

What qualifies a person to be a leader of "We the People?" What characteristics should we, as Christians, look for in the people we nominate and elect? For the most part, we have gone about this process the wrong way for quite some time. In terms of looking at candidates for political service, we look mostly at policy. What policies, or how many policies, do the candidate and I share that would allow me to be able to vote for him/her. Then, after we have determined where he/she sits on the political spectrum, we sometimes look to his/her character. There are even times where we skip this step altogether if we feel that the candidate is that good of a politician. What if we inverted the way that we looked at these men/women who aspire to serve us? What if we looked at each candidate first as a person? That is not to say policy is unimportant, as it shares a root with politics and that is what we are discussing. That being said, what if we examined the character traits of the nominees and narrowed down the field to those who met the standards to which we, at the very least, hold ourselves? Instead of looking at them as a politician first and person second, we should look at them as a person first and a politician second. Is there a chance that we would find ourselves with a field of men/women who we would be proud to say represent us as citizens? It is also very possible that by looking at the state of a candidate's character, first, we would often find that the people we hold in high character also share many of our same policy ideals.

Sadly, we have recently fallen further and further away from a nation that has religion at its very core and woven throughout the fabric of its creation. It was not that long ago, in the Presidential election of 1952, that Republican candidate Dwight D. Eisenhower said, "In spite of the difficulties of the problems we have, I ask you this one question: If each of us in his own mind would dwell more upon those simple virtues- integrity, courage, self-confidence, an unshakable belief in his Bible- would not some of these problems tend to simplify themselves?"[1] At the same time, Democratic candidate Adlai Stevenson promised as he accepted the party's nomination, "to do justly and to love mercy and walk humbly with my God."[2] Today, we, unfortunately, see many different candidates that scoff at God's law and shrug off the very principles that are discussed in His word.

When determining who to nominate and elect in elections, the ultimate goal should be to determine the "good guys" and the "bad guys." How can a person make such a determination? In his book "How Do You Kill 11 Million People," Andy Andrews asks this very question. He follows up that question with this subsequent question, "Would truth be a starting point for telling the difference"?[3] In this book, Mr. Andrews looks at the event of the Holocaust and how such an egregious act was allowed to happen. He asserts that men like Adolf Hitler and Adolf Eichmann were able to promote such crimes against humanity simply because of their large, continuous lies. Obvi-

---

1. Barber 1992, 268.
2. Ibid.
3. Andrews 2011, 47.

ously, honesty cannot be the only factor for differentiating between good and bad. A murderer could be honest when asked
if he killed someone, but his honesty alone doesn't make him
good. However, it is fair to say that a person's honesty could
be a good starting point for determining the goodness of his/
her character. It is up to us, as the American public, to determine such goodness as we choose these officials. This may
sound like a utopian idea to some. It has long been said, often
truthfully, that all politicians lie. That being said we must stop
using that as an out for continuing to put such people in posi-
tions of power. It is us who are empowered to hold these men/
women accountable for the lies that they do tell. We must stop
using the "both sides do it," or "it's just politics" arguments. We
must instead, begin to hold the people who we put in public office to the high standards to which we strive to hold ourselves.

The two-party system in American politics has crippled
our way of thinking for quite some time. It has molded us into
thinking of politics in binary terms. A person is either Republican or Democrat, on the left or the right. In doing this, we
have become politically more tribal with each passing year.
You must affiliate yourself with one team or the other, and you
must be all in on said team or tribe. If you are on the right, you
must love everything said by the right and hate everything said
by the left. If you disagree with someone within your tribe or
you say that someone on the other side has a good idea, then
you are not legitimate. You are not a true member of the team.
This is not only not conducive to nominating and electing the
right people, but it forces us to put candidates into categories
that are not at all backed up by any scriptural, moral, or ethical
standards. It has forced us to measure our politicians on the
spectrum of left and right instead of on the spectrum of right
and wrong.

In the book of Exodus, we see that Moses was chosen by
God to lead the people of Israel out of captivity in Egypt. Af-

ter the ten plagues and the miraculous safe crossing of the Red Sea, Moses found himself in charge of a great multitude of people. In Exodus 18 Moses' father-in-law, Jethro, watched Moses govern over the people. After seeing that Moses had taken on this responsibility all by himself, Jethro offered him advice for how he could choose leaders among the people to delegate some responsibilities. How could he decide who was fit to govern the people?

> "Listen now to my voice; I will give counsel, and God will be with you: Stand before God for the people, so that you may bring the difficulties to God. And you shall teach them the statutes and the laws, and show them how they must walk and the work they must do. Moreover, you shall select from all the people able men, such as fear God, men of truth, hating covetousness; and place such over them to be rulers of thousands, rulers of hundreds, rulers of fifties, and rulers of tens. And let them judge the people at all times. Then it will be that every great matter they shall bring to you, but every small matter they themselves shall judge. So it will be easier for you, for they will bear the burden with you. If you do this thing, and God so commands you, then you will be able to endure, and all this people will also go to their place in peace" (Exodus 18:19-23).

In his book, "God and Government," Dave Miller provides a commentary on these verses. He elaborates on the critical qualities of good political leaders that Jethro has spoken to Moses in this passage of scripture. He says,

"First, the population must be taught God's laws and God's way. Government should facilitate-not hinder-that necessity. Second, the people must select political leaders who (1) are capable, i.e., savvy, informed, intelligent, and familiar with their governmental responsibilities; (2) fear God, i.e., they have a healthy respect for God and seek His approval, unwilling to do anything that would bring God's disfavor; (3) are truthful, i.e., they are honest and would never deceive the people, mislead them, or misrepresent the facts; and (4) hate greed, i.e., they do not seek office in order to advance their own financial standing and they do not act in their public capacity out of self-interest".[4]

The question we must ask ourselves is, "Do we hold our elected officials to these standards?" The beauty of our American Republic is that we have been empowered to set the standard and hold our leaders to such a standard, but have we been doing so? One may notice that the qualities listed here are a perfect blend of high-character people of God as well as people who are intelligent and informed with the inner workings of government. It is true that simply being a good person does not qualify one to be a political leader, but neither does just being a good politician. Unfortunately, we have only looked at the characteristics of the latter for decades.

Founding Father, Noah Webster, had this to say about choosing the right people for public office:

"When you become entitled to exercise the right of voting for public officers, let it be impressed on your mind that God commands you

---

4. Dave Miller 2017, 66.

to choose for rulers, just men who will rule in fear of God. The preservation of a republican government depends on the faithful discharge of this duty; if the citizens neglect their duty, and place unprincipled men in office, the government will soon be corrupted; laws will be made, not for the public good, so much as for selfish or local purposes; corrupt or incompetent men will be appointed to execute laws; the public revenues will be squandered on unworthy men; and the rights of the citizens will be violated or disregarded. If a republican government fails to secure public prosperity and happiness, it must be because the citizens neglect the divine commands, and elect bad men to make and administer the laws. Intriguing men can never be safely trusted."[5]

It should be the goal of a Christian to nominate and elect people to public office that are striving to carry out Godly policy and are also men/women of high character. A Christian should never be able to vote for someone who would be in favor of policy that goes against God's law and His will, and a Christian must also make sure that he/she doesn't give any politician a pass on character issues simply because he/she will vote the way we want them to. We must remove ourselves from the binary, tribal mindset of choosing public officials and we must strive to find not only the best politician but the best person for the job. Those politicians may be few, but they are out there, and we must give them our support. We must also encourage other good, Christian people to run for public office when the opportunity presents itself. Yes, the world of politics may be riddled with liars and cheaters, but how much could we

---

5.   Webster 1832, 307-308.

move forward as a nation if we worked collectively to remove those trends from our states and from Washington? How much easier would it be to re-incorporate the missing Biblical world-view into politics if we only nominated and elected leaders that held to that same world-view? We could find ourselves one step closer to "One Nation under God" once again.

3

ABORTION

With a topic as controversial as this one, many different points must be made. The first is that being pro-life does not imply that one must also be anti-woman. A Christian should feel just as strongly about a woman's rights as they do a man's. Galatians 3:28 says, "There is neither Jew nor Greek, there is neither slave nor free, there is neither male nor female; for you are all one in Christ Jesus." That being said, abortion has nothing to do with a woman's right to choose, or not choose, pregnancy. There are many women all across the United States (and the world) who would choose pregnancy if that was an option for them. I personally (and I am sure you do as well) know people who have been blessed by adoption, but it was in large part because they were unable to get pregnant. It is not that they didn't choose pregnancy; it's that pregnancy didn't choose them. Both male and female have a right to choose how they treat their body; however, the "right to choose" line is drawn when it involves another body, no matter how small or newly formed. A woman does not always get to choose when to become pregnant, but she can choose when not to become pregnant, with the only exception being rape which we will address later in this chapter. When it comes to a woman's right to choose to end the life of her child, at any stage of her pregnancy that is not a right that any Christian should stand behind because God does not stand behind it.

WHAT DOES THE BIBLE SAY?

The Bible has a lot to say about babies and children. In Luke 1:41 it says, "And it happened, when Elizabeth heard the greeting of Mary, that the babe leaped in her womb; and Elizabeth was filled with the Holy Spirit." How could something with no moral or intrinsic value perform such an act? In Jeremiah 1:5 it says, "Before I formed you in the womb I knew you; before you were born I sanctified you; I ordained you a prophet to the nations." Clearly God had a plan for Jeremiah before he was ever an embryo, fetus, or born. Notice what the beginning of the verse says, "Before I formed you..." Who are we to destroy what is the innocent handiwork of the Creator?

In Matthew 18 Jesus speaks to the disciples about little children when they ask him, "Who then is greatest in the kingdom of heaven?" Christ answers in Matthew 18:3-4 and says, "Assuredly, I say to you, unless you are converted and become as little children, you will by no means enter the kingdom of heaven. Therefore whoever humbles himself as this little child is the greatest in the kingdom of heaven." Furthermore, in Matthew 19:14 Jesus shows His love for the innocence of a child when He says, "Let the little children come to Me, and do not forbid them for of such is the kingdom of heaven." A child is one of the most innocent of all of God's creation no matter if he/she is newly formed in the womb or a toddler. Christ showed His love towards them, but the Bible also speaks against them that wish to do harm to the innocent, including children. In Deuteronomy 27:25 the old law states, "Cursed is the one who takes a bribe to slay an innocent person. And all the people shall say, Amen!" Also in Proverbs 6:16-19 it says, "These six things the Lord hates, yes, seven are an abomination to Him: A proud look, a lying tongue, hands that shed innocent blood, a heart that devises wicked plans, feet that are swift in running to evil, a false witness who speaks lies, and one who sows discord among brethren."

How could any Christian, knowing these things, go to a voting booth and willingly support a candidate or party platform that looks to protect or enhance the institution of abortion? The Bible is the greatest truth that has ever been written, and we need look no further than it as a guide for our lives. That being said, the Bible was not written as a scientific guide for the start of human life, but as a guidebook for the saints on their journey to heaven and to help sinners come to repentance. There is a great deal of science that speaks on abortion and human life, and it is important to view this issue from that perspective as well.

WHAT DOES SCIENCE SAY?

Anyone who has ever witnessed or been a part of childbirth can attest that this amazing process is something that only the Creator could control and dictate. From the moment a male sperm combines to fertilize the female egg, a separate and unique human being begins to take shape. It is a scientific fact that from this conception there is a new organism that exists that was not in existence before. This new being is equipped with his/her own DNA that is different from that of both the mother and the father. This DNA is obviously and distinctly human as the offspring of two species is always the same as the parents. Not only does this child have his/her own DNA, but it also has a gender. The male sperm carries either an X or a Y chromosome to the female's X chromosome. If it is the male's X chromosome, then the child is a girl (XX), and if it is the male's Y chromosome, then the child is a boy (XY). How could one proclaim that an organism with human DNA and a gender does not already have moral and intrinsic value? In Keith L. Moore's scientific textbook, The Developing Human: Clinically Oriented Embryology, the beginning of human life is further defined:

> "A zygote [fertilized egg] is the beginning of a new human being. Human development begins at fertilization, the process during which a male gamete ... unites with a female gamete or oo-cyte ... to form a single cell called a zygote. This highly specialized, totipotent cell marks the beginning of each of us as a unique individual."[1]

Within the first trimester of the pregnancy, this little child is already growing and maturing at a rapid rate. The image in Appendix B shows the development of a fetus through all the stages of his/her life. The first row alone shows the development through the first trimester. Notice all the developments in these first twelve weeks. Yet, there are still some who declare that the unborn child is not living during this development stage. Science says otherwise.

> "Although it is customary to divide human development into prenatal and postnatal periods, it is important to realize that birth is merely a dramatic event during development resulting in a change in environment."[2]

It is clear both from the scriptures and science that it is the Lord that determines when life begins. It is the Creator who is the author of life, yet man has seen fit to create his own time-

---

1. Moore and Persaud 2003, 16.
2. Ibid., 1.

table which determines human existence. The fact is, any time a line is drawn to signify the beginning of human existence, other than that of conception, it can be easily defeated when applied to an adult human.

WHAT DOES THE COURT SAY?

The two main Supreme Court cases that broke the federal government's silence on this topic are Griswold v. Connecticut and Roe v. Wade. The more well-known of these two cases is Roe v. Wade (1973), as it is known across the country as the case that changed the abortion laws in 46 U.S. states. Griswold v. Connecticut is, in fact, not a case that deals with abortion, but the ruling in this case played a drastic outcome in the ruling of Roe v. Wade. The Griswold case happened in 1965 and dealt with Estelle Griswold, the Executive Director of the Planned Parenthood League, who was, along with the Medical Director of the League, giving information and instruction to married couples regarding birth control. This violated a Connecticut law and ultimately posed this question: Does the Constitution provide martial privacy against state restrictions on a couple's ability to be counseled in the use of contraceptives? The Court ruled that although the Constitution does not have an explicit "right to privacy" clause, it can be inferred using the First, Third, Fourth, and Ninth Amendments, and then that right is delegated to the states using the 14th Amendment.[3] This case plays a major role for abortion because it is later cited by members of the Court in Roe v. Wade and plays a key role in that case decision.

Fast forward eight years to 1973, and you arrive at the Roe v. Wade case. Jane Roe was a Texas resident who looked to terminate her pregnancy via abortion. Under Texas law this

3. Griswold v. Connecticut 1965.

act was illegal except for when the health of the mother was in danger. Roe challenged the Constitutionality of this law, and the Court prepared itself to answer the following question: Does the Constitution embrace a woman's right to terminate her pregnancy by abortion? Ultimately the Court held that a woman's right to an abortion fell under her right to privacy that was recognized in Griswold v. Connecticut. This landmark decision gave women total control over their pregnancy during the first trimester and defined different levels of state interest for the second and third trimester.[4]

The problem with cases, such as the two mentioned above, is that they come to very wrong conclusions when asked simple questions. A Constitutional right to privacy (federal or state) found in the Griswold case should not play any role in the question asked in Roe v. Wade. The Constitution does not embrace a woman's right to terminate her pregnancy via abortion because the Constitution does not protect anyone's right to murder under Title 18 of the United States Code.[5] In fact, In 2004 the Unborn Victims of Violence Act was passed by the 108th Congress as an amendment to Title 18 of the United States Code. It was in this amendment that an embryo or fetus was recognized as a legal victim if injured or killed. Furthermore, this amendment defines a child in utero as a member of the Homo-sapiens species at any stage of development who is carried in the womb.[6]

In 2004, presidential Democratic candidate John Kerry, who voted against the bill as a senator, is quoted as saying, "I have serious concerns about this legislation because the law cannot simultaneously provide that a fetus is a human being and protect the right of the mother to choose to terminate

---

4.   Roe v. Wade 1973.
5.   18 U.S. Code § 1111 n.d.
6.   Congress 2004.

her pregnancy."[7] Mr. Kerry was not wrong in his statement. Although the law does provide for exceptions for abortions and other medical procedures, it is difficult to see how that could be possible. How could a child carried in the womb, at any stage of development, be defined as a member of the human race in one sentence and then the next sentence protect a woman's right to kill that child through abortion. Simply put, our lawmakers got it right when they applied the correct scientific and biblical definition of life to a child in the womb and the abortion exception is in complete contradiction with that life. Murder is murder no matter who commits the act. When it is unwanted (i.e. the killing of mother and child by someone else) and when it is wanted (the killing of a child by his/her mother). Both constitute as murder since an innocent life is being taken. When a person kills a mother and child, he/she makes a choice. It is the wrong choice, but it is his/her choice. The mother makes the same wrong choice when she chooses to kill her unborn child.

WHAT ABOUT RAPE?

One of the largest elephants in the room during the discussions about abortion is rape. Rape is a nasty and vile thing, and it is often cited as a reason to allow abortion. Even many political conservatives allow for the rape exemption when laying out their abortion stance. So, should a Christian stand against abortion even when rape is involved? The short answer, yes. There is no denying that rape is an atrocity. It is a heinous act and those who commit such things should receive the proper justice. That being said, justice is not found in taking the innocent life of a child, and to do so violates God's will.

Rape is the only instance in which a woman truly has zero

7.   Robinson 2007.

say in what has happened to her body. In every other instance that can be cited, she may not have wanted to become pregnant at a given time, but ultimately she did have partial control over that outcome. In the event of rape, however, that is not the case. So how is it fair that a woman's body can be hijacked by pregnancy, completely against her will, and she can do nothing about it? It's not. It is truly unfortunate, and I feel for any woman in those circumstances. That being said, it is also not fair when a woman's body is hijacked by cancer, completely against her will. It is not fair when a young girl's body is hijacked as they begin their menstrual cycle, completely against their will. It is not fair when a woman's body is hijacked for any reason one can imagine, but the killing of an innocent unborn child does not suddenly make it fair either. One may argue, "But if you could do something to stop cancer then you would," and that may be true, but I dare say he/she would not go as far as to take another human life in order to do so.

The rape exemption is often listed as a justifiable cause for abortion, but the numbers show that abortions that are carried out due to rape-induced pregnancies are actually extremely low. According to the Guttmacher Institute, there were 926,200 abortions in 2014 (the most recent year of data at the time of this writing).[8] This number was actually down from three years prior where the number was recorded by the same group to be over one million. According to the Statista report of crime and law enforcement data, there were 84,864 reported forcible rape cases in the year 2014.[9] Granted, not all rape cases are reported each year, but that is the data that is available. Of course, not all instances of rape result in pregnancy. A study that was published in 1996 by the American Journal of Obstetrics and Gynecology indicated that the national rape-re-

8.   Guttmacher Institute n.d.
9.   Statista n.d.

lated pregnancy rate among woman of reproductive age (12-45) was 5.0 percent.[10] This study surveyed 4,008 adult women over a three year period. Ultimately there were 315 victims of rape and 20 of those victims became pregnant as a result of this rape. This study estimated that over a year's time, there would be roughly 32,000 rape-related pregnancies. One of the researchers, Dean Kilpatrick, said in an interview cited by the Washington Post in June 2013 that when adjusted to today's population that number would be about 50,000 rape-related pregnancies a year.[11]

In 2004 the Guttmacher Institute conducted a study in which it surveyed 1,209 women who had decided to have an abortion asking them the main reason for their decision to do so. This survey was passed out at nine separate abortion clinics throughout the country. Of the women surveyed, less than 0.5 percent stated that they had an abortion because they were a victim of rape. Percentages were the highest (23% and 25% respectively) in the categories of "Can't afford a baby" or "Not ready for a child."[12] Furthermore, the state of Florida records a reason for every abortion that happens within its state borders. In 2015 there were 71,740 cases of abortion in Florida. Of those cases, a mere .085% stated that they were having an abortion because they were a victim of rape.[13]

What conclusion do these numbers bring us to? There were 926,200 abortions in 2014 and 84,864 reported cases of rape in the same year. Dean Kilpatrick, one of the researchers for the American Journal of Obstetrics and Gynecology study, stated that with an adjustment to today's population, estimations could be set at around 50,000 rape-related preg-

---

10. Melisa M. Holmes 1996.

11. Kessler 2013.

12. Abort 73 2018.

13. Ibid.

nancies in a year. Yet, according to the Guttmacher survey of post-abortion women and the Florida statistics of reason for abortion within their state, abortions occur at a frequency of less than 1.0% due to being a victim of rape. If we even raised that number to an even 1.0%, that would mean that of the 50,000 rape-related pregnancies in the U.S. only 500 of them have resulted in abortion. So of the 926,200 abortions in the year 2014, roughly only 500 of them were because the woman was a victim of rape. That leaves 925,700 abortions in the United States in 2014 that took place for a reason other than rape.

The fact is, although it is often cited by many pro-choice groups throughout the country, the rape exemption does not really exist. A much higher percentage of all abortions in the United States are a result of some other instance. As already mentioned, rape is the only case in which the woman has zero say in what is happening to her body. Yet, the numbers show that abortions happen at a much greater frequency when this uncontrollable factor of rape is not at play.

****

Even taking into account the incident of rape, as a Christian it is extremely important to be consistent in our viewpoints. If abortion is murder in one instance, then it is murder in every instance. Are there unfortunate circumstances such as rape and the declining health of the mother? Absolutely. Nonetheless, human life begins at conception, and to willingly and knowingly terminate that innocent life for any reason would constitute as the unlawful and sinful act of murder.

4

GENDER

When I was a kid, my brothers and I had an extensive Lego collection. I don't know if they are nearly as popular today, but back then I know that all of my friends had them by the thousands. It seemed that Legos were on our Christmas list every year. We had a Tupperware box full of them with all different shapes and sizes. Whenever it came time for us to construct something out of these Legos, we would dump them all out on the floor so that we could easily find every piece that we needed. Sometimes we would follow an instruction booklet, and other times we would build something from our imagination. When our "Lego Monster" was finally finished, I remember looking upon it with great satisfaction and joy. I had created that. Hours before, there was just a floor full of colorful blocks, and now I had given value and purpose to my creation. I had shown my superiority over the Legos.

While using Legos as an example of creation may be a bit silly, I believe it is safe to say that you can understand the point. A creator is greater than his creation. Sadly, we live in a world where so many of the created think that they are better than their Creator. Now they may not come out and say such a thing, but it is clearly shown in their actions. The fourth word of the book of Genesis introduces us to our Creator, and the rest of that book (and the whole Bible) show us His power. Genesis 1:1 says, "In the beginning God created the heavens and the earth." Have you ever truly stopped to think about this? The same God that created all of the heavens and all of the earth created us! Genesis 1:27 reads, "So God created man in His own image; in the image of God He created him; male and female He created them." If God is the creator of both man and woman, and the Creator is greater than His creation, then why are so many bringing into question how God created them?

In Psalms 139:14, David wrote, "I will praise You, for I am fearfully and wonderfully made; marvelous are Your works, and that my soul knows very well." David understood that he was wonderfully made by a Creator that was greater than himself. How can man, who was created from the dust of the ground (Gen. 2:7) and woman who was created from man (Gen. 2:21-23) think that they can do a better job of deciding what they are than He who created them? The Creator gives purpose and value to creation. If we read through all of Genesis chapter one, we can see that God created nothing without a purpose. Who are we to challenge Him?

Outside of the scripture, there is also science to back the differences between male and female. Notice these two statements from both a scientific textbook and the National Human Genome Research Institute:

> "In that fraction of a second when the chromosomes form pairs, the sex of the new child will be determined, hereditary characteristics received from each parent will be set, and a new life will have begun."[1]
>
> "The human genome is organized into 23

1.	Kaluger and Kaluger 1979, 54.

pairs of chromosomes (22 pairs of autosomes and one pair of sex chromosomes), with each parent contributing one chromosome per pair. The X and Y chromosomes, also known as the sex chromosomes, determine the biological sex of an individual: females inherit an X chromosome from the father for a XX genotype, while males inherit a Y chromosome from the father for an XY genotype (mothers only pass on X chromosomes). The presence or absence of the Y chromosome is critical because it contains the genes necessary to override the biological default - female development - and cause the development of the male reproductive system."[2]

The issue of gender identification is not up to us, as humans, to discern. The Creator made us in His image. Nothing that we feel or want can change His work. Sadly, I feel a large portion of this comes from the idea of people in this world wanting to be "different." There is nothing wrong with being different in this world. In fact, God calls upon all of His children to be different from the world. In 2 Corinthians 6 He tells us, "....Do not be unequally yoked together with unbelievers" and further He says, "...come out from among them and be separate, says the Lord." The difference here is that we are to be different, not so people will look at us, but so that people will look at Him. People in our world say, "I want to be different, but I don't want to be treated differently." This just makes no sense. As Christians, we know that we are different, but we know full well that we will be treated differently and that to be expected (John 15:18-21).

---

2.   Roseanne F. Zhao 2014.

God is the Great Creator. His work is masterful and it is without mistake. The moment we begin to question God's ability to make things is the moment we start to question His power and ability to be our God, neither of which is a wise decision. Thank God that the Creator is greater than His creation, for I know it is a task that we could not handle. "Because the foolishness of God is wiser than men, and the weakness of God is stronger than men" (1 Corinthians 1:25).

GENDER ROLES

What about gender roles? Society has a lot to say about the roles of both men and women. Men should not be too "masculine" as to make themselves superior over women, especially not their wives. Women must make sure that they are not too submissive to men so that they do not become inferior to their male counterparts. The person, not the Creator, is the one who determines what gender he/she identifies with, and if they don't like it, then they can change. This may be how much of the world sees gender, but what does the Bible say?

Unlike the world, God's word is much more specific on the topic of men and women. We have already mentioned Genesis 2:7, but let's read what it says. "And the Lord God formed man of the dust of the ground, and breathed into his nostrils the breath of life; and man became a living being." Further, in verses 22-23, it says, "Then the rib which the Lord God had taken from man He made into a woman, and He brought her to the man. And Adam said: 'This is now bone of my bones and flesh of my flesh; she shall be called woman, because she was taken out of man.'" God created both man and woman and it was He, the Creator, who decided their gender then, and it is He who decides our gender now.

How should men and women act? The Bible actually has much to say about this topic. In 1 Timothy we read of the qualifications of elders (or bishops) in the church. I dare say these characteristics should be what every man uses as the guidelines for his life. 1 Timothy 3:2-7 reads, "A bishop then must be blameless, the husband of one wife, temperate, sober-minded, of good behavior, hospitable, able to teach; not given to wine, not violent, not greedy for money, but gentle, not quarrelsome, not covetous; one who rules his own house well, having his children in submission with all reverence (for if a man does not know how to rule his own house, how will he take care of the church of God?); not a novice, lest being puffed up with pride he fall into the same condemnation as the devil. Moreover he must have a good testimony among those who are outside, lest he fall into reproach and the snare of the devil."

When it comes to women, the Bible spends an entire chapter on this in the book of Proverbs. Proverbs 31 has much to say about a virtuous woman, but let's take a moment to look at verses 26-31. It reads, "She opens her mouth with wisdom, and on her tongue is the law of kindness. She watches over the ways of her household, and does not eat the bread of idleness. Her children rise up and call her blessed; her husband also, and he praises her; 'Many daughters have done well, but you excel them all.' Charm is deceitful and beauty is passing, but a woman who fears the Lord, she shall be praised. Give her of the fruit of her hands, and let her own works praise her in the gates."

What about men and women together? "Wives, submit to your own husbands, as is fitting in the Lord. Husbands, love your wives and do not be bitter toward them" (Colossians 3:18-19). The Bible says plenty about men and women. It clearly lays out how gender is determined, and it clearly lays out the roles of both men and women in the home. How much easier things would be if we looked to the Bible for answers to our questions. So often it tells us all we need to know.

Finally, in his 2014 article, "Male and Female Roles: Gender in the Bible," Dave Miller closes with this thought that I believe fully encompasses the biblical teachings of gender roles throughout scripture. He says,

> "A final word needs to be said concerning the fact that both men and women must remember that Bible teaching on difference in role in no way implies a difference in worth, value, or ability. Galatians 3:28 ("neither male nor female"), 1 Timothy 2:15 ("she shall be saved"), and 1 Peter 3:7 ("heirs together of the grace of life") all show that males and females are equals as far as their person and salvation status is concerned. Women are often superior to men in talent, intellect, and ability. Women are not inferior to men anymore than Christ is inferior to God, citizens are inferior to the President, or church members are inferior to elders."[3]

TOXIC MASCULINITY?

There are many different viewpoints in society about the concept of masculinity. Some think that the definition is found in appearance, as they see a man who is strong, grows a full beard, and according to some commercials, drinks Dr. Pepper 10. Others view masculinity as a toxic behavior that encompasses all of the negative behaviors of men such as infidelity, sexism, and in some cases, rape. With all of that said, how can we know the definition of true masculinity, and how can we, as men, aspire to it, and as women, seek it out in a spouse?

It is evident throughout the scriptures that biblical masculinity is not found in the outward appearance. Although it is found within a man's actions, I believe that we need to be careful not to emasculate men simply because of the terrible neg-

---

3.   Dave Miller, Male and Female Roles: Gender in the Bible 2014.

ative actions of some men in society. The author C.S. Lewis made mention of this in his book, The Abolition of Man, when he said, "We make men without chests and expect from them virtue and enterprise. We laugh at honor and are shocked to find traitors in our midst."[4] True masculinity must be rooted in God's word. It must pursue honor and virtue in all aspects and interactions of life.

In 1 Timothy 5:8 it says, "But if anyone does not provide for his own, and especially for those of his household, he has denied the faith and is worse than an unbeliever." A man of God looks to be the provider in his home. This is not just the provisions of monetary value, but of love, sacrifice, service, and wisdom. Notice in Ephesians 5:25 it says, "Husbands, love your wives, just as Christ also loved the church and gave Himself for her." Furthermore, in verses 28-29 it reads, "So husbands ought to love their wives as their own bodies; he who loves his wife loves himself. For no one ever hated his own flesh, but nourishes and cherishes it, just as the Lord does the church." Looking back in Proverbs 4:10-15 it reads, "Hear, my son, and receive my sayings, and the years of your life will be many. I have taught you in the way of wisdom; I have led you in right paths. When you walk, your steps will not be hindered, and when you run, you will not stumble. Take firm hold of instruction, do not let go; keep her, for she is your life. Do not enter the path of the wicked, And do not walk in the way of evil. Avoid it, do not travel on it; turn away from it and pass on."

Christ gave Himself for the church through His sacrifice, and a man of God should look to show this type of sacrificial love to his wife and family. True masculinity is found in servant-leadership where the man leads his family as the head of the home (Eph. 5:23-24) through his service and sacrifice to them. A man of God also looks to pass on the wisdom of God's

---

4.   Lewis 1944, 8.

word to his children. He understands the importance of his example and wants to impart the wisdom that he has learned through the scriptures to every generation of his house. He knows that success is found in those who live their life and go to heaven and he wants to do his part to ensure that success for all of those who bear his family name.

Micah 6:8 says, "He has shown you, O man, what is good; and what does the Lord require of you but to do justly, to love mercy, and to walk humbly with your God?" We must begin to redefine masculinity with the Bible instead of with the misconceived views of society. God made man in His image, and He intended for man to use his masculinity to protect his house and spread the good news of His word to each passing generation. As a man, you should strive to be as those men of God that are described in His word, and as a woman you must settle for nothing less than a man who looks to uphold God's definition of masculinity.

****

Ultimately, the entire concept of gender is left up to God, not man. Men and women are equal in the sight of the Lord in terms of their soul and value, but they were designed intrinsically different from one another. Men were designed to protect, and women were designed to nurture. Having these differences does not make one better than the other, but instead makes them the perfect match.

5

HOMOSEXUALITY

Same-sex marriage and homosexuality will probably be a controversial issue for some time to come. It has been talked about more and more in the past few years and will likely be an issue in many political campaigns in the future. It is important to point out that a Christian does not hate homosexuals just as God does not hate them. The Bible, however, is very clear about how God feels about the act of homosexuality and therefore same-sex marriage. Churches and Christians everywhere will be confronted by this issue, and they need to know what the Bible says. This is a topic that many in the world, and even in the church, have begun to conform to because it is just easier to get along. We must remember the importance of consistency and understand that the path of least resistance is never the one we should take if it means we go against God's word. For Christians who accept the Word of God as the ultimate authority in their lives, the answer lies in the Bible. What does it say regarding same-sex marriage and homosexuality?

WHAT DOES THE BIBLE SAY?

First, let's look at some Old Testament references of same

sex marriage and homosexuality. For expediency we will not read through every passage in the text, but they will be listed for you to look at on your own. The most well-known case of this in the Old Testament is the Sodom incident in Genesis 19:1-13. Here, God destroyed an entire city because of their homosexuality. Homosexuality has always been a sin according to God's truth. In Leviticus 18:22, it says, "You shall not lie with a male as with a woman. It is an abomination." Further in Leviticus 20:13, God condemns this once again when he says, "If a man lies with a male as he lies with a woman, both of them have committed an abomination. They shall surely be put to death. Their blood shall be upon them." These are just a few of the Old Testament examples with others being found in Judges 19:15-25 and 1 Kings 14:24.

As Christians we now live under the Christian Age and not under the Law of Moses found in the Old Testament, so are all of these Old Testament passages irrelevant? No. We look at the passages in the Old Testament to show that from the very beginning God has abhorred the idea of same-sex marriage and homosexuality. God has always been and will always be consistent in His truth.

The New Testament also references the sin of homosexuality multiple times. In Romans 1:26-27, it says, "For this reason God gave them up to vile passions. For even women exchanged the natural use for what is against nature. Likewise also the men, leaving the natural use for what is against nature, burned in their lust for one another, men with men committing what is shameful, and receiving in themselves the penalty of their error which was due." Notice that it discusses men leaving the natural use of a woman to be with another man. This tells us that it is unnatural and therefore is not a state that we are born into. We see this further shown in 1 Corinthians 6:9-10 where it says, "Do you not know that the unrighteous will not inherit the kingdom of God? Do not be deceived. Neither fornicators, nor idolaters, nor adulterers, nor homosexuals, nor sodomites, nor thieves, nor covetous, nor drunkards, nor revilers, nor extortioners will inherit the kingdom of God." How plain is this scripture in listing homosexuals as those who will not inherit the kingdom of God? We must not water down the truth! We can read in 1 Timothy 1:10 that sodomites (those who practice homosexuality) are contrary to sound doctrine, and another reference to Sodom and Gomorrah is in Jude 1:7 as it discusses them going "after strange flesh." The facts are simple and easily laid out in the scripture for us to see. God always has been and always will be against homosexuality.

Of course many arguments have been made over the years for the approval of homosexuality in today's society. Some may say, "The Bible is outdated in this way and no longer applies as times have changed." If we apply that principle to this concept, then we have thrown out the idea of an absolute truth. The Bible is God breathed (2 Timothy 3:16), and there is no fault that can be found in it. Another argument is, "Homosexuals were born this way, and God would not condemn them for how He made them." First, we can see from some of the previous scriptures we have noted that it is described as unnatural, and secondly, if homosexuals cannot inherit the kingdom of Heaven (as we have read), would God create a human for the purpose of going to hell?

Another argument may be, "This is what makes me happy, and God would want me to be happy." So often people fall into this trap of trying to interpret how God would want them to be. They feel that they know God well enough that they know what he wants. This is something that we need to always remember: our happiness becomes irrelevant when it starts to interfere with God's will for our lives. Does God want us to be happy? Sure he does, but more than ANYTHING else, God wants us to be saved. Any temporary sadness we may face on this earth will be well worth the reward we receive by doing His will.

When discussing this topic, it really is not nearly as difficult as so many try to make it. We cannot fit the square peg into the round hole just to suit our wishes. God is clear and plain when discussing these topics. The wonderful thing about the standard by which we are judged is that it is absolute. We have absolute truth in His word (John 17:17). We know as Christians that we are to keep the truth pure according to Proverbs 23:23, "Buy the truth, and do not sell it, Also wisdom and instruction and understanding." If we are serious about keeping God's truth pure, we cannot change it to fit the world, culture, or a particular lifestyle. All of those things must instead yield to the absolute truth of God and His word. He discusses marriage and He discusses what a proper marriage looks like. God determines what constitutes a proper marriage, not man. We must always remember that marriage is a divine institution, not a civil one, and marriage throughout the Bible is always between a man and a woman. Same-sex marriage is totally foreign to the Bible and to the doctrine of Christ. The only marriage that is approved by God is between a male and a female. The sanctity of this marriage has been and will continue to be under attack. Some may say, "Love is personal and don't we want love to win out? Is God not all about love?" All of these statements are true. The problem is that no love should be more important in our lives than God's. Love truly wins when our love for God trumps all else. We are to love the Lord with all our heart, soul, and mind as read in Mark 12:30 and put Him high above all else. Without a true and sincere love for God, no one has ever really loved at all because, "He who does not love does not know God, for God is love" (1 John 4:8). Let's let love win!

Love wins when love is perfected. How can this be? Love is perfected when we love Him because He first loved us. We read in 1 John 4:17-19, "Love has been perfected among us in this: that we may have boldness in the Day of Judgment; because as He is, so are we in this world. There is no fear in love;

but perfect love casts out fear, because fear involves torment. But he who fears has not been made perfect in love. We love Him because He first loved us." We will not fear when love is perfected because a perfect love of God keeps His commandments (John 14:15). Yes, we will make mistakes and sin just as everyone does, but to live habitually in sin is not showing a love for God. We are to love our brother (1 John 4:20-21), but we will not love his sin because we know that sin separates us from God (Isaiah 59:2), and to be separated from God is not to love Him. 1 John 1:5-7 says, "This is the message which we have heard from Him and declare to you, that God is light and in Him is no darkness at all. If we say we have fellowship with Him, and walk in darkness, we lie and do not practice the truth. But if we walk in the light as He is in the light, we have fellowship with one another, and the blood of Jesus Christ His Son cleanses us from all sin."

WHAT DOES THE CONSTITUTION SAY?

Not only is homosexual marriage not biblical, but it is also not Constitutional, at least not at the national level. The only argument for the Constitutionality of same-sex marriage is the use of the 14th Amendment. Those in favor of same-sex marriage say that if it is not allowed then the government is in violation of both the Equal Protection Clause and the Due Process Clause of the 14th Amendment. However, when read and understood within the context in which this Amendment was written, this is not true. Section I of the Fourteenth Amendment says:

> "All persons born or naturalized in the United States, and subject to the jurisdiction thereof, are citizens of the United States and of the State wherein they reside. No State shall make

or enforce any law which shall abridge the privileges or immunities of citizens of the United States; nor shall any State deprive any person of life, liberty, or property, without due process of the law; nor deny to any person within its jurisdiction the equal protection of the laws."

This was proposed by Congress in 1866 in the year following the American Civil War, and it was ratified by the states in 1868. It followed the Thirteenth Amendment, ratified in 1865, which had abolished slavery. The Fourteenth Amendment, along with the Thirteenth and Fifteenth, are all three post-Civil War slavery amendments. That was the conversation that was being had during this time of our nation's history. No part of the Fourteenth Amendment was to be extended to the rights of homosexuals to marry. How can we know this? Because in 1868 when this amendment was ratified among the states, it was against the law, in every state, not only for same-sex couples to marry, but for anyone to participate in a homosexual act (both publicly and privately).[1] In fact, up until 1961, when Illinois changed its criminal law, it was a felony in all 50 states to participate in a homosexual act.[2] How is it possible then, that if all the states in 1868 had a state law criminalizing homosexuality, that they would turn around and ratify an Amendment to the U.S. Constitution that could ultimately permit it? Simply put, that was not at all their intention. We must understand history and our Constitution within the context of the time period in which it was written.

Another example of this would be to look at both amendments fifteen and nineteen. There are three times in the orig-

---

1.   Turek 2015.

2.   HISTORY OF SODOMY LAWS AND THE STRATEGY THAT LED UP TO TODAY'S DECISION n.d.

inal seven articles of the Constitution where it talks about voting. Article I Section II talks about the people voting for members of the House of Representatives, Article I Section III talks about state legislatures voting for Senate members, and Article II Section I talks about the a group of electors (electoral college) voting for the President. In Article I Section II, the exact wording is as follows:

> "The House of Representatives shall be composed of Members chosen every second Year by the People of the several States, and the Electors in each State shall have the Qualifications requisite for Electors of the most numerous Branch of the State Legislature."

The wording of "people of the several states" is very vague, and if the Constitution was to change with the times and norms of society, there would be absolutely no need for the Fifteenth and Nineteenth Amendments. The fact is, "the people of the several states" that are described in Article I Section II are, of course, talking about a small group of people: most often white-male landowners. Congress knew that in its original form, Article I Section II did not include women or African-Americans, and therefore, in order to give them the right to vote, the Constitution had to be amended.

The Fourteenth Amendment, within historical context, does not include the rights of homosexuals to be married. It is a matter that should and must be left up to the states according to the 10th amendment. Our Constitution is indeed a living document. Our founders created it that way when they wrote the amendment process into Article Five. In order to create a national same-sex marriage law, Congress and the states must add the twenty-eighth amendment to the Constitution.

HOW THE COURTS GOT IT WRONG

The majority of the Supreme Court drastically misinterpreted the use of the Fourteenth Amendment as they ruled on the Obergefell v. Hodges case in 2015. The fundamental questions of this case were 1) Does the Fourteenth Amendment require a state to license a marriage between two people of the same sex? 2) Does the Fourteenth Amendment require a state to recognize a marriage between two people of the same sex that was legally licensed and performed in another state? The court ruled yes to both of these questions in a 5-4 decision.[3]

The dissenters of this case, Justices Scalia, Thomas, Alito, and Chief Justice Roberts understood both the purpose of the Fourteenth Amendment and the power of the court in this case, but unfortunately, they were overruled as five of the members of the most powerful court in the land enacted legislation that exceeded their scope and power. Chief Justice John Roberts says in his dissent:

> "Whether same-sex marriage is a good idea should be of no concern to us. Under the Constitution, judges have power to say what the law is, not what it should be. The people who ratified the Constitution authorized courts to exercise "neither force nor will but merely judgment." The Federalist No. 78, p. 465.
>
> Although the policy arguments for extending marriage to same-sex couples may be compelling, the legal arguments for requiring such an extension are not. The fundamental right to marry does not include a right to make a State change its definition of marriage. And a State's

---

3.   Obergefell v. Hodges 2015.

decision to maintain the meaning of marriage that has persisted in every culture throughout human history can hardly be called irrational. In short, our Constitution does not enact any one theory of marriage. The people of a State are free to expand marriage to include same-sex couples, or to retain the historic definition....

Understand well what this dissent is about: It is not about whether, in my judgment, the institution of marriage should be changed to include same-sex couples. It is instead about whether, in our democratic republic, that decision should rest with the people acting through their elected representatives, or with five lawyers who happen to hold commissions authorizing them to resolve legal disputes according to law. The Constitution leaves no doubt about the answer."[4]

Chief Justice Roberts points out the exact points, as I mentioned before, that the issue of same-sex marriage is left solely up to the states, and the federal courts have absolutely no authority to change this legislation. Such a change is left to Congress, or the states, who have the ability to propose an amendment to the Constitution.

Justice Antonin Scalia furthered the Chief Justice's points in his own dissent when he said:

"...It is not of special importance to me what the law says about marriage. It is of overwhelming importance, however, who it is that rules me. Today's decree says that my Ruler, and the Ruler of 320 million Americans coast-to-coast, is

---

4.   Ibid.

THE POLITICAL CONSCIENCE OF THE CHRISTIAN

a majority of the nine lawyers on the Supreme Court. The opinion in these cases is the furthest extension in fact—and the furthest extension one can even imagine—of the Court's claimed power to create "liberties" that the Constitution and its Amendments neglect to mention. This practice of constitutional revision by an unelected committee of nine, always accompanied (as it is today) by extravagant praise of liberty, robs the People of the most important liberty they asserted in the Declaration of Independence and won in the Revolution of 1776: the freedom to govern themselves.

Until the courts put a stop to it, public debate over same-sex marriage displayed American democracy at its best. Individuals on both sides of the issue passionately, but respectfully, attempted to persuade their fellow citizens to accept their views. Americans considered the arguments and put the question to a vote. The electorates of 11 States, either directly or through their representatives, chose to expand the traditional definition of marriage. Many more decided not to. Win or lose, advocates for both sides continued pressing their cases, secure in the knowledge that an electoral loss can be negated by a later electoral win. That is exactly how our system of government is supposed to work.

...When the Fourteenth Amendment was ratified in 1868, every State limited marriage to one man and one woman, and no one doubted the constitutionality of doing so. That resolves these cases. When it comes to determining the meaning of a vague constitutional provision—

such as "due process of law" or "equal protection of the laws"—it is unquestionable that the People who ratified that provision did not understand it to prohibit a practice that remained both universal and uncontroversial in the years after ratification. We have no basis for striking down a practice that is not expressly prohibited by the Fourteenth Amendment's text, and that bears the endorsement of a long tradition of open, widespread, and unchallenged use dating back to the Amendment's ratification. Since there is no doubt whatever that the People never decided to prohibit the limitation of marriage to opposite-sex couples, the public debate over same-sex marriage must be allowed to continue."[5]

****

God's perspective on same-sex marriage and homosexuality has never wavered since the time when He created man. In Genesis 1, God created man, and in Genesis 2, He saw that it was not good for man to be alone, and he made woman from the rib of man. Soon after that, we have record of the first marriage in Genesis 2:24 where it says, "Therefore a man shall leave his father and mother and be joined to his wife, and they shall become one flesh."

Our founders created a Constitution that allowed for its citizens to define marriage within their respective state; however, a true Christian has always known this definition, and it should never change because God has never and will never change.

---

5.   Ibid.

SOCIAL & ECONOMIC EQUALITY

How does Christianity fit into a conversation about socialism, capitalism, and societal egalitarianism? Capitalism, or a free market, and Christianity go hand in hand because both require action. In a socialistic society, someone can gain by doing absolutely nothing at all. Capitalism is a meritocracy; you are rewarded for your deeds. Certainly some have an easier road than others, but in no other system can one rise to prominence faster and with less interference than in capitalism. While our admission into heaven is not a meritocracy, the Bible is clear that there is still action to be done. We are saved by both grace and faith, and our faith is proved by our works.

A great example of this can be seen in Ephesians 2:8-10. It reads, "For by grace you have been saved through faith, and that not of yourselves; it is the gift of God, not of works, lest anyone should boast. For we are His workmanship, created in Christ Jesus for good works, which God prepared beforehand that we should walk in them." Notice that it says that we are saved by grace through faith. Our faith is proved through our works. Grace is God's gift to the world, and it is our job to accept it through our faith.

Think of it this way: It is your birthday and I have decided to give you a new pair of shoes. I wrap the box and hand it to you as a gift, but you don't yet know what it is. You tell me thank you, but then you set the box, still wrapped, off to the side and forget about it. It gets lost in the shuffle of the day, and you never actually open it. Do you actually have a new pair of shoes? The answer is, of course, no. Although I gave you the gift, you never opened it. God supplies us with the gift of his grace, but He leaves it up to us to open the gift through our faith. This "living/working faith" is seen in James 2:17-26. It reads, "Thus also faith by itself, if it does not have works, is dead. But someone will say, 'You have faith, and I have works.' Show me your faith without your works, and I will show you my faith by my works. You believe that there is one God. You do well. Even the demons believe- and tremble! But do you want to know, O foolish man, that faith without works is dead? Was not Abraham our father justified by works when he offered Isaac his son on the altar? Do you see that faith was working together with his works, and by works faith was made perfect? And the Scripture was fulfilled which says, 'Abraham believed God, and it was accounted to him for righteousness.' And he was called the friend of God. You see then that a man is justified by works, and not by faith only. Likewise, was not Rahab the harlot also justified by works when she received the messengers and sent them out another way? For as the body without the spirit is dead, so faith without works is dead also." Furthermore, Matthew 7:21 reads, "Not everyone who says to me, 'Lord, Lord,' shall enter the kingdom of heaven, but he that does the will of My Father which is in heaven." There is something that we must do.

Christianity holds the individual accountable, not the group as a whole. Romans 14:12 says that we must each give an account of ourselves. People work hard in capitalism because they are working for their own reward. They know that their output is largely dependent on their input. When you take away the incentive of a profitable output because you spread the wealth around to others, then the input is greatly reduced. Think for a moment if you had to answer on judgement day for the whole world (or even just for your local community). As you went through your daily life and looked around at the evil in which people participate, you begin to lose hope. In the same way, why would anyone ever feel a desire to make their life right with the Lord if they felt that their sins could be covered by the Godly life of another? Eventually, everyone would be waiting for others to fill in the spiritual gaps for them because living worldly is seen as much more fun.

The following is an analogy that I use in my classroom with my students every year when we are discussing the concept of fair and equal. I once read something similar online, but in my research I have never found the originality of this story, and I am not sure if it is indeed based on true events, but it proves the point at hand:

I tell my students that my classroom is capitalistic in nature. Everyone has the same opportunity to do well. They receive the same notes, the same book, and the same test, but the outcome for each of them is not the same. That is fair, but it's not equal. I then tell them to pretend for a moment that I used the socialist model in my classroom. I gave them the same notes, book, and test, but the outcome for each of them was not the same. Half of the class studies hard and gets an A, while the other half of the class slacks off and gets an F. In an effort to be fair and equal, I tell them that I am going to average all of their grades together so that they receive equal outcomes. Therefore, everyone in the class gets a C. Now, the students who originally got an F are pumped. They tell all their friends that this is the best class ever! However, the students who originally made an A are quite upset. They are not pleased that their hard work and study were ultimately taken from them, at least in part. As the next test rolls around the slackers continue their slacking ways and make another F. The students who made an A on the first test are a bit discouraged, but they still care, and they make a B. In an effort to be fair and equal, I average all of the grades together again and everyone gets a D. Again, half of the class is pleased while the other is not at all. As this continues the slackers continue to make F's and the high performing start to become more and more discouraged. They are tired of working hard just to have it taken from them and given to someone else. They try to tell the slackers to pull their weight and perhaps they could take turns on who does well so that the class average will be higher, but once you have continually received something without working for it, why would you start working now? At the end of the semester, the entire class has failed, and there are a great deal of people upset. What I was doing was equal, but it sure wasn't fair! Ultimately, the point is proven. Fair and equal are not the same thing.

The truth is, capitalism is the only system that works in a democracy of a free people. That is why it has been the economic system used in the United States since its inception even though it is not specifically stated in our founding documents. It doesn't have to be stated because a free society cannot operate any other way. Alexis de Tocqueville, a French diplomat who toured the nation in the 1830's and published his findings in the well-known book, "Democracy in America," once said, "Democracy extends the sphere of personal independence; socialism confines it. Democracy values each man at his highest; socialism makes each man an agent, an instrument, a number. Democracy and socialism have but one thing in common- equality. But note well the difference. Democracy aims at equality in liberty. Socialism desires equality in constraint and in servitude."[1]

---

1. Dave Miller, God and Government 2017, 86.

WHAT'S MINE IS YOURS

What about the less fortunate? As a Christian people, we should have a love and compassion for our fellow man because we see them as a soul. We should have a desire to help them when possible. We should not, however, be forced into doing so through government intervention. Matthew 25:34-46 explains the importance of giving to those less fortunate, but a Christian does so out of the kindness of his heart, not because government has made such an act mandatory. Why? Because ultimately doing so promotes theft. When something is taken against your will, even if it is done so by the government, that is theft.

Think about this analogy: What if I walked outside and noticed that one of my neighbors had two riding lawn mowers in his garage? As I noticed my other neighbor's garage, I saw that he had only a basic push-mower. I know my neighbors well, and they are both nice people. In an effort to help out the "push-mower" neighbor, I take one of the riding mowers from the other neighbor and give it to him. Although I was trying to do an act of goodwill, it is obvious what has just happened. I have stolen from one neighbor to give to the other. If the government steps in and forces one neighbor to give a riding mower to the other so that they are equal, it doesn't change the fact that theft has occurred. If, however, the neighbor with two riding mowers wants to give one to his less fortunate neighbor, then that is his prerogative because he can do what he wishes with his property. It all comes down to a God-given right to property.

Do we have such a God-given right to property? We perhaps remember from our high school history classes that the Enlightenment thinker, John Locke, listed the natural rights of life, liberty, and property. We remember that Thomas Jefferson, in his writing of the Declaration of Independence changed these words to life, liberty, and the pursuit of happiness. Did the Founders not see the same value in property as Locke did? Or did they not see it as a fundamental, God-given right? On the contrary. The idea of the pursuit of happiness was in direct connection with the ability to own property.

John Adams, who served on the Declaration committee with Thomas Jefferson, among others, had this to say about private property.

> "The moment the idea is admitted into society that property is not as sacred as the laws of God, and that there is not a force of law and public justice to protect it, anarchy and tyranny commence. Property must be secured or liberty cannot exist."[2]

In the scope of American government, socialism, or the redistribution of wealth/goods, goes against the basis of the founding of the nation as a whole. Supreme Court Justice George Sutherland made this point in a speech he once gave to the New York state bar association.

> "It is not the right of property which is protected but the right to property. Property, per se, has no rights; but the individual- the man- has three great rights, equally sacred from arbitrary interference: the right to his LIFE, the right to his LIBERTY, the right to his PROPERTY... The three rights are so bound together as to be essentially one right. To give a man his life but deny him his liberty, is to take from him all that makes his life worth living. To give him his liberty but

---

2.   Skousen 1981, 174.

take from him the property which is the fruit and
badge of his liberty, is to still leave him a slave."[3]

We can also look at numerous verses throughout scripture
that point to a God-given right to property. We see this concept going all the way back to the Ten Commandments given
to Moses. The 8th commandment listed in Exodus 20:15 says,
"You shall not steal." What is there to steal if no person owns
any property himself? Furthermore, the 10th commandment
in Exodus 20:17 says, "You shall not covet your neighbor's
house; you shall not covet your neighbor's wife, nor his male
servant, nor his female servant, nor his ox, nor his donkey, nor
anything that is your neighbor's." Notice the final few words of
this commandment, "that is your neighbor's." It is his property
granted to him by God above.

Fast forward to the New Testament, and we see this same
concept. In Acts 5:1-4, the apostle Peter condemns a man by
the name of Ananias along with his wife, Sapphira. They lied
when they said that they sold all of what they had and gave the
proceeds to the church. Notice how Peter refers to their property. "But a certain man named Ananias, with Sapphira his wife,
sold a possession. And he kept back part of the proceeds, his
wife also being aware of it, and brought a certain part and laid
it at the apostles' feet. But Peter said, 'Ananias, why has Satan
filled your heart to lie to the Holy Spirit and keep back part of
the price of the land for yourself? While it remained, was it not
your own? And after it was sold, was it not in your own control?
Why have you conceived this thing in your heart? You have
not lied to men but to God.'" Their sin was not in their lack of
donating their whole property but in lying about it in order to
seem righteous.

It is the fundamental and God-given right to property that

---

3. Ibid., 173.

makes the redistribution of wealth mindset not only against the laws created by our Founders but against the natural laws created by God himself. While a Christian should be willing to help his fellow man in need, he cannot be forced to do so, nor should he do so on a continual basis as to make his fellow man dependent upon his help. The Bible is clear when it speaks of one's command to strive to be self-sufficient. "For even when we were with you, we commanded you this: If anyone will not work, neither shall he eat" (2 Thessalonians 3:10).

Perhaps former President Grover Cleveland said it best when he stated his reasons for vetoing legislation that was created with the purpose of spending federal tax dollars for private welfare.

> "I can find no warrant for such an appropriation in the Constitution, and I do not believe that the power and duty of the General Government ought to be extended to the relief of the individual suffering which is in no manner properly related to the public service or benefit. A prevalent tendency to disregard the limited mission of this power and duty should, I think, be steadfastly resisted, to the end that the lesson should be constantly enforced that though the people support the Government the Government should not support the people.
>
> The friendliness and charity of our countryman can always be relied upon to relieve their fellow-citizens in misfortune. This has been repeatedly and quite lately demonstrated. Federal aid in such cases encourages the expectation of paternal care on the part of the Government and weakens the sturdiness of our national character, while it prevents the indulgence among our people of that kindly

sentiment and conduct which strengthens the bonds of a common brotherhood."[4]

THE BIBLE & SOCIETAL EGALITARIANISM

I once heard a denominational preacher rightly say, "Too many people are under the impression that societal egalitarianism is the primary goal of the gospel." Egalitarianism by definition is the belief in the equality of all people, especially in political, social, or economic life. Too often people see the love and kindness that Christians are to show towards others as them being advocates of egalitarianism, but according to scripture that is simply not the case.

To promote such an idea, some will often quote a various verses in Leviticus. For example, Leviticus 19:10 which says, "And you shall not glean your vineyard, nor shall you gather every grape of your vineyard; you shall leave them for the poor and the stranger: I am the Lord your God." Or perhaps they will quote Leviticus 25:35-37, "If one of your brethren becomes poor, and falls into poverty among you, then you shall help him, like a stranger or a sojourner, that he may live with you. Take no usury or interest from him; but fear your God, that your brother may live with you. You shall not lend him your money for usury, nor lend him your food at a profit." The problem with using verses such as these is that it is a quotation of old law, which we as Christians, are no longer bound too. That is not to say that the Old Testament is therefore irrelevant to Christians. The old law is useful to us as Christians, but not as something we are to follow (which we discuss more later in the chapter). Frankly, we should be thankful that we are no longer bound to the Law of Moses. An in-depth look at the book of Leviticus will show us some quite serious laws and consequences for

4.   Ibid., 177.

violating them. Let us look at a few.

- Leviticus 19:27-28- "You shall not shave around the sides of your head, nor shall you disfigure the edges of your beard. You shall not make any cuttings in your flesh for the dead, nor tattoo any marks on you: I am the Lord."

- Leviticus 20:9-10- "For everyone who curses his father or his mother shall surely be put to death. He has cursed his father or his mother. His blood shall be upon him. The man who commits adultery with another man's wife, he who commits adultery with his neighbor's wife, the adulterer and the adulteress, shall surely be put to death."

- Leviticus 20:13- "If a man lies with a male as he lies with a woman, both of them have committed an abomination. They shall surely be put to death. Their blood shall be upon them."

- Leviticus 20:27- "A man or a woman who is a medium, or who has familiar spirits, shall surely be put to death; they shall stone them with stones. Their blood shall be upon them."

So, if the old law is no longer the standard by which Christians are held, what good is it to us, and how can we know for sure that we no longer live under it. In Romans 7:7 Paul says, "What shall we say then? Is the law sin? Certainly not! On the contrary, I would not have known sin except through the law. For I would not have known covetousness unless the law had said, 'You shall not covet.'" Furthermore, in Romans 15:4 it says, "For whatever things were written before were written for our learning, that we through the patience and comfort of the Scriptures might have hope." It is clear from these passages that it still certainly serves a purpose for us as Christians, but how can we be certain that we no longer live under this old law? This is found in Galatians 3:19-25. It reads, "What purpose then does the law serve? It was added because of transgressions, till the Seed should come to whom the promise was made; and it was appointed through angels by the hand of a mediator. Now a mediator does not mediate for one only, but God is one. Is the law then against the promises of God? Certainly not! For if there had been a law given which could have given life, truly righteousness would have been by the law. But the Scripture has confined all under sin that the promise by faith in Jesus Christ might be given to those who believe. But before faith came, we were kept under guard by the law, kept for the faith which would afterward be revealed. Therefore the law was our tutor to bring us to Christ, that we might be justified by faith. But after faith has come, we are no longer under a tutor."

But what about the New Testament? It may be evident that we are no longer under the old law that is laid out in Leviticus and Deuteronomy, but surely if we live under the new law and covenant (as described in Hebrews 8:7-13), the New Testament says something about societal egalitarianism? There are certain passages that, when taken out of context, seem to agree with this sentiment. However, when put in their proper place in the scripture within the context of what is being said or taught, that is simply not the case. Let's look at some examples.

In Luke 14:12-14 it reads, Then He also said to him who invited Him, 'When you give a dinner or a supper, do not ask your friends, your brothers, your relatives, nor rich neighbors, lest they also invite you back, and you be repaid. But when you give a feast, invite the poor, the maimed, the lame, the blind. And you will be blessed, because they cannot repay you; for you shall be repaid at the resurrection of the just.'" Prior to this passage Christ is reminding those with Him to remain humble in all things. He reminds them in verses 7-11 not to think themselves higher than they are. The verses following (verses 15-24), Christ gives the Parable of the Great Supper. The point of this parable is that the gospel is for all. Those that still see themselves as the "chosen people" of God will not be invited to taste the supper of Christ. That would be a lesson in and of itself, but the point is made that the original verses do not equate to Christ promoting societal egalitarianism.

Another scripture from the New Testament that is often used is 1 John 3:17. It reads, "But whoever has this world's goods, and sees his brother in need, and shuts up his heart from him, how does the love of God abide in him?" To fully understand this verse it is important to read the passage that comes directly before it in verse 16. "By this we know love, because He laid down His life for us. And we also ought to lay down our lives for the brethren." The "brother" and "brethren" that is being discussed here are those who are in Christ and His church. We are certainly to look after one another and help one another because we are a family in Christ. Galatians 6:10 furthers this point as it says, "Therefore, as we have opportunity, let us do good to all, especially to those who are of the household of faith." This; however, does not support the claim that Christ was in favor of a societal egalitarianism for all. It does not even support the claim that He was for such a thing among those in the church. It simply states that if you have goods to help a fellow brother in Christ who is in need, you must do so, yet it does not support the idea of economic, social, or political equality.

Finally, in Paul's letter to the Christians at Rome, he reminds them of how a Christian is to act. In Romans 12:9-21 it says, "Let love be without hypocrisy. Abhor what is evil. Cling to what is good. Be kindly affectionate to one another with brotherly love, in honor giving preference to one another; not lagging in diligence, fervent in spirit, serving the Lord; rejoicing in hope, patient in tribulation, continuing steadfastly in prayer;

distributing to the needs of the saints, given to hospitality. Bless those who persecute you; bless and do not curse. Rejoice with those who rejoice, and weep with those who weep. Be of the same mind toward one another. Do not set your mind on high things, but associate with the humble. Do not be wise in your own opinion. Repay no one evil for evil. Have regard for good things in the sight of all men. If it is possible, as much as depends on you, live peaceably with all men. Beloved, do not avenge yourselves, but rather give place to wrath for it is written, 'Vengeance is Mine, I will repay,' says the Lord. Therefore 'If you enemy is hungry, feed him; if he is thirsty, give him a drink; for in so doing you will heap coals of fire on his head.' Do not be overcome by evil, but overcome evil with good." It is important to note that nowhere in this part of scripture, or in any other part of the New Testament, does it say that a Christian should be working to help provide societal egalitarianism for all those he comes in contact with.

All men are created equal. When Thomas Jefferson penned these words in the Declaration of Independence his intention was not to mean that all men are created with equal intellect, status, or physical prosperity. They are created as beings by God, and are equal in the sight of God. They are all born free and independent, no matter what political, economic, or societal class on earth they were born into. Nowhere in scripture does it say that eradicating our worldly inequalities is a biblical goal. We are to be good stewards of all we have, and we are to be kind, loving, and giving to our fellow man. However that kindness and love does not advocate a handing out of things simply because some are less fortunate on this earth than others. Christ told us to be servants. He took on the form of a servant Himself. On earth, He was a nobody, He reigns today as our King. Earthly status was never part of His ministry. It was about preparing oneself for eternity. Ultimately, poverty and hardship will always be a byproduct of this world because the devil and sin are a prominent part of this world. The role of a Christian, according to the gospel of Christ, is to help prepare the eternal soul, above all else. In doing so we are to show compassion and love to others. We show the love of God by being loving towards others; however, that love is through the gospel of Christ and the power that it has to save souls. Not through the equality of status or things.

The good news is that this life is but vapor that passes away (James 4:14). Christ tell us in John 16:33, "These things I have spoken to you, that in Me you may have peace. In the world you will have tribulation; but be of good cheer, I have overcome the world." Further in 1 John 5:4 it says, "For whatever is born of God overcomes the world. And this is the victory that has overcome the world—our faith." Victory and equality are not found in material possessions, but in Him.

7

GUNS

There are passages in both the Old and New Testaments that are worth our consideration in regards to this issue. In Genesis 4:8-11, it says, "Now Cain talked with Abel his brother; and it came to pass, when they were in the field, that Cain rose up against Abel his brother and killed him. Then the Lord said to Cain, 'Where is Abel your brother?' He said, 'I do not know. Am I my brother's keeper?' And He said, 'What have you done? The voice of your brother's blood cries out to Me from the ground. So now you are cursed from the earth, which has opened its mouth to receive your brother's blood from your hand."

This is the first ever recorded murder in the history of the world, and yet, something is missing from this account. What did Cain kill Abel with? A rock perhaps? Or maybe he merely strangled him to death. Notice that the Bible does not record the weapon or means that Cain used to kill Abel, nor does God ask Cain about his weapon of choice when He confronts him. Why is this relevant? Because the weapon itself murdered no one. The emphasis here is not on the means of killing but on the personal responsibility that falls on the killer for his actions.

In the New Testament in Luke 22:36-38 it says, "Then He said to them, 'But now, he who has a money bag, let him take it, and likewise a knapsack; and he who has no sword, let him sell his garment and buy one. For I say to you that this which is written must still be accomplished in Me: And He was numbered with the transgressors. For the things concerning Me have an end.' So they said, 'Lord, look, here are two swords.' And He said to them, 'It is enough.'" Notice that Christ tells his apostles to equip themselves with a lethal weapon. This is not because he wants them to go out and attack others, but because he knows that because of their faith in Him, they may have to defend their own lives. Christ permits the apostles to defend themselves physically with the use of carnal weapons.

Just as throughout scripture, the Founders knew the importance of the right to keep and bear arms to preserve the defense of one's self and household. The Englishman, Sir William Blackstone, whose writing "The Commentaries on the Laws of England," had a dramatic impact on the foundations of American government said the following:

> "The fifth and last auxiliary right of the subject, that I shall at present mention, is that of having arms for their defence, suitable to their condition and degree, and such as are allowed by law...and is indeed a public allowance, under due restrictions, of the natural right of resistance and self-preservation, when the sanctions of society and laws are found insufficient to restrain the violence of oppression"[1]

Furthermore, American patriot Thomas Paine said:

> "The peaceable part of mankind will be continually overrun by the vile and abandoned, while they neglect the means of self defence.

---

1. Dave Miller, God and Government 2017, 27.

The supposed quietude of a good man allures the ruffian; while on the other hand, arms like laws discourage and keep the invader and the plunderer in awe, and preserve order in the world as well as property."[2]

Many have said that it is sad that we have reached a point in society when we must carry weapons out of fear. While this may be the case for some, I do not believe it to be the case for most. People carry a gun, go to the range, and practice shooting just in case a situation ever arises, they can say that they were prepared. For the same reasons, we read our Bible. We study God's word, we look to grow in the faith, and "sharpen our sword." Why? Because we are preparing for heaven, for evangelism, and to defend God's truth if the situation arises. 1 Peter 3:15 says, "But sanctify the Lord God in your hearts, and always be ready to give a defense to everyone who asks you a reason for the hope that is in you, with meekness and fear."

The world is full of evil and sinful people. It is a sad truth, and unfortunately, as long as the devil exists, these people will continue to exist. That is why some have chosen to prepare themselves in all aspects of life to defend the things that are most dear, and I am thankful that our Founders thought it necessary to protect such a right. It is not mandated in the scripture (nor in the Constitution) do to so by carrying a physical weapon, but it is certainly permitted.

It is, however, mandated in scripture that those who proclaim Christ carry the powerful weapon that is the Word of God. Ephesians 6:11 says, "Put on the whole armor of God, that you may be able to stand against the wiles of the devil." Further, in verse 17 we read, "And take the helmet of salvation, and the sword of the Spirit, which is the word of God." The

---

2. Ibid. 28.

weapon of His word is the only weapon we are to use for the cause of Christ in furthering His kingdom. "For the word of God is living and powerful, and sharper than any two-edged sword, piercing even to the division of soul and spirit, and of joints and marrow, and is a discerner of the thoughts and intents of the heart" (Hebrews 4:12).

The Bible speaks of weapons that are both carnal and spiritual in nature. While carrying carnal weapons is permitted for a defense of our physical body, carrying the spiritual weapon of God's word is a requirement for those who profess Christ. Carrying a firearm (or any weapon), just as carrying God's word, is not about fear but preparation. In the same manner, Christians can't live their lives in fear of death, but they must carry the knowledge of God's word so that they can be prepared when death may come.

For the same reasons, I read my Bible. I study God's word, I look to grow in the faith, and "sharpen my sword." Why? Because I am preparing for heaven, for evangelism, and to defend God's truth if the situation arises.

Our Founders knew that you could not legislate all sinful behavior; however, what you can do is prepare yourself in all aspects of life to defend the things that are most dear. I don't live my life in fear of being attacked. That's not why I carry. I carry to be prepared if an attack may come. Comparatively, I don't live my life in fear of death; nevertheless, I carry the knowledge of God's word with me so that I can be prepared when death does come.

One of the main arguments that many will make against the Second Amendment today is that the Founders did not intend for us to have semi-automatic weapons. This is simply not true. In fact, when the Second Amendment was enacted, the regular civilian had a military-grade weapon. He carried the same type and caliber of weapon as an army soldier. The Second Amendment does not say that citizens have the right to bear muskets. It says they have the right to bear arms. Yet, in today's world, there have even been regulations put on certain military-grade firearms that are restricted from civilian purchase. One cannot claim that it was never the Founder's intention to own such weapons. If that is the case, then the same argument could be made about the First Amendment. Upon the inception of the First Amendment, such things as telegraphs, telephones, the internet, Facebook, and Twitter did not exist. Yet, they are all protected under the First Amendment because the Bill of Rights does not simply protect the things that were available in 1791.

The argument is often further made that the purpose of "right to keep and bear arms" was created solely for use for local militias. Yet, that is also not the case. Don B. Kates who is a scholar and historical researcher on the Second Amendment says the following:

> "The 'militia' was the entire adult male citizenry, who were not simply allowed to keep their own arms, but affirmatively required to do so.... With slight variations, the different colonies imposed a duty to keep arms and to muster occasionally for drill upon virtually every able-bodied white man between the age of majority and a designated cut-off age. **Moreover, the duty to keep arms applied to every household, not just to those containing persons subject to militia service. Thus the over-aged and seamen, who were exempt from militia service, were required to keep arms for law enforcement and for the defense of their homes."**[3] (emp. added)

As Christians and Americans, we have a God-given right

3.   The James Madison Research Library and Information Center n.d.

to self-defense. God's word authorizes the use of weapons to provide such a defense, and the Founders of our Constitution took it upon themselves to maintain that right as they drafted it as the Second Amendment to the Bill of Rights.

CONCLUSION

This book is meant to be both thorough and concise in its explanation of the issues with which Christians may come in contact as they actively participate in American politics. It is not meant to be an exhaustive list, but hopefully, it can help steer the reader in the right direction as they vote and make political decisions as American citizens.

As a United States history and government teacher, I love to study the history of this great nation. It is fascinating to read and learn about the men and women who came before us, the things that they did and the price that some of them paid. Founding Fathers, Presidents, entrepreneurs, military leaders, civil rights leaders and so many more shaped the country that we know today. I honestly feel that we owe a great debt to those men and women. They went through more than we'll ever know or could ever imagine.

In my studies, however, I have noticed one common denominator between many of these great Americans of the past, God. So many of these great men and women knew that as long as we put God first as a nation, then everything else would take care of itself. Sadly, I believe that we lose more and more of our heritage with each passing year. So many have strayed from the Biblical principles upon which this nation was founded. Yes, we could blame the government, but in a democratic republic, is it not the people who are to blame? After all, we are the ones who elect our representatives. This reminds me of the people in 1 Samuel 12. They had begged God for a king, and He finally agreed to give them one, but He left them with something to remember. Verses 13-15 read, "Now therefore, here is the king whom you have chosen and whom you have desired, and take note, the Lord has set a king over you. If you fear the Lord and serve Him and obey His voice, and do not rebel against the commandment of the Lord, then both you and the king who reigns over you will continue following the Lord your God. However, if you do not obey the voice of the Lord, but rebel against the commandment of the Lord, then the hand of the Lord will be against you, as it was against your fathers."

Sometimes, I think we forget what Jesus tells us in Mark 16. "Go into all the world and preach the gospel to every creature. He who believes and is baptized will be saved; but he who does not believe will be condemned." Are we doing this, or do we need to put our boots on the ground and get to work? There has never been a more important campaign in the history of the world than one that emphasizes the greatness of God. This world is a scary place, but I thank God that this world is not my home. I know that I have a home in Heaven, and I want to put all my focus on getting to Heaven and getting as many people to go with me as I can.

On July 30, 1956, President Dwight D. Eisenhower signed a law officially declaring "In God We Trust" to be the nation's official motto. This same law also mandated that the phrase be printed on all American paper currency. Fast forward to the present day, and we are a much different country than we were in 1956. The idea of "In God We Trust" as our country's official motto has been debated for years by various secular groups. Nonetheless, the motto remains and desires our sincere observation.

Do we understand the power in saying the simple phrase "In God We Trust?" Many people today say this phrase flippantly without realizing what is actually being said. We, as a nation, put our trust in God knowing that through Him, and with reliance upon Him, we can do all things (Phil. 4:13). We say, "In God we trust" but, the question should be asked, do we really? What if we did? Psalms 33:12 says, "Blessed is the nation whose God is the Lord, the people He has chosen as His own inheritance." You and I can't answer for the entire nation as a whole, but we can answer for ourselves. Do you and I really trust in God? Are we doing our part in this nation to put our trust in Him? Psalm 144:15 says, "Happy are the people who are in such a state; happy are the people whose God is the Lord!"

What a nation we could be if we decided to be people who really do trust in God. What a nation we could be if we prayed regularly and followed the infallible truth that is God's word. What a nation we could be if God came first and all other things came after. 1 Peter 2:9 describes His people, His church, His nation. "But you are a chosen generation, a royal priesthood, a holy nation, His own special people, that you may proclaim the praises of Him who called you out of darkness into His marvelous light." What if, as a country, we strove to be a part of that nation? A nation that truly trusts in Him. A nation that could say proudly, with no reservations, "In God We Trust!" I pray that we move towards that type of nation. We must all do our part.

POLITICAL CORRECTNESS

Political correctness is a prevalent part of American society. By definition it is: conforming to a belief that language and practices which could offend political sensibilities should be eliminated. Ultimately, the roots of this idea can be found in three basic principles: 1.) Don't offend me 2.) Love=tolerance

3.) It's okay as long as it makes me happy. One would think that the Bible would have a lot to say on these subjects. After all, a Christian should never set out to personally offend someone, love is an integral part of being Christ-like, and Christians should be the happiest people on earth. So, let's take a moment to see what the Gospel has to say on these issues.

1. Don't offend me: Christ never made it His mission purposely to offend those around Him, but He also knew that the truth would be found as offensive to some. Throughout His life, Jesus was concerned with pleasing God only. In John 8:29 He says, "And He who sent Me is with Me. The Father has not left Me alone, for I always do those things that please Him." Paul made this same point in Galatians 1:10 when he said, "For do I now persuade men, or God? Or do I seek to please men? For if I still pleased men, I would not be a servant of Christ." The Bible is clear: although we shouldn't intentionally be offensive, we should concern ourselves with pleasing God and not pleasing men.

2. Love=tolerance: In recent years the world has drastically misunderstood the word love. God's word has much to say on the topic. 1 Corinthians 13:4-8 describes the characteristics of love, and tolerance is not one that is listed. Christ knew that loving someone meant being honest with them and not tolerating their poor behavior. In Mark 10:17, a rich young man was asking Christ what it took to inherit eternal life. Jesus gave the man a list of things in verse 19 when he said, "You know the commandments: 'Do not commit adultery, Do not murder, Do not steal, Do not bear false witness, Do not defraud, Honor your father and your mother." The rich young man was excited and said, "Teacher, all these I

have observed from my youth." Clearly, it seemed that this was a good man. Christ could have easily told him that he was good enough, but notice what it says in verse 21, "Then Jesus, looking at him, loved him, and said to him, 'one thing you lack: Go your way, sell whatever you have and give to the poor, and you will have treasure in heaven; and come, take up the cross, and follow Me.'" Christ was honest with this man because He loved him. He knew that in his current state he was not fit for the Kingdom of Heaven, but that he could be, and he needed to know the truth. Christ knew that true love=honesty, not tolerance.

3. It's okay as long as it makes me happy: As Christians, we should be the happiest people on earth because we know that we have the hope of heaven. That being said, if our "happiness" ever contradicts our salvation, then the choice of which to choose should be easy. We must know that God is not concerned with our happiness; He is concerned with our soul. 1 Timothy 2:4 says, "Who desires all men to be saved and to come to the knowledge of the truth." We must not get wrapped up in our own happiness and become like the seed that fell among the thorns in Luke 8:14. "And the ones that fell among thorns are those who, when they have heard, go out and are choked with cares, riches, and pleasures of life, and bring no fruit to maturity." The Bible is clear: your happiness is empty if it is not tied to your salvation.

Political correctness is tolerant and inoffensive. The Gospel of Christ is infallible and perfect. It is impossible for something as pure as God's word to be politically correct. In Romans 12:18, it says, "If it is possible, as much as depends on you, live peaceably with all men." We should strive to follow this principle, but we must never compromise God's truth. We must never conform to the world's values and definitions but transform that world with the values and definitions of Christ.

SINGLE-ISSUE VOTER

One of the greatest arguments against the Christian voter is that we are single issue voters. We focus on only one issue (in many cases, abortion) and disregard the rest. The problem with this argument is that I dare say that everyone, to a certain extent, is a single issue voter. Everyone who develops their own political ideology does so around certain key issues. Everyone has specific issues that they care about more than others. Perhaps for some, it is abortion, but for others, it may be taxes, immigration, the economy, etc. There are key issues that are held in higher regard to all those who are active in American politics. These are their non-negotiables. These are their "single-issues." As a Christian, there should no doubt be certain issues that are non-negotiable as we make our political decisions. Many of them are outlined in this book. The Bible is clear when it speaks about many of these things, and to go against His word on these issues, in the name of politics, places our citizenship to this country higher on the priority list than our citizenship to His Kingdom.

In 1957, when President Dwight D. Eisenhower was inaugurated into office for his second term, he placed his hand on Psalm 33:12 as he took the oath of office. This verse reads, "Blessed is the nation whose God is the Lord, the people He has chosen as His own inheritance." We must always remember that God must come first in all things.

I love these United States just as I know that you do. We truly do live in a blessed nation. However, above all else, we need to remember that, as Christians, we have dual citizenship. Most importantly we are citizens of heaven. Philippians 3:20 says, "For our citizenship is in heaven, from which we also eagerly wait for the Savior, the Lord Jesus Christ..." Yes, we do live in a great nation, but I am thankful that we serve a God that has prepared a far greater place. A place that you and I, as Christians, can call home. A place that we can hope for and yearn for. A place that no man, government, military or anything else can destroy. That beautiful place called heaven, where God's people are citizens.

"Do not lay up for yourselves treasures on earth, where moth and rust destroy and where thieves break in and steal; but lay up for yourselves treasures in heaven, where neither moth nor rust destroys and where thieves do not break in and steal. For where your treasure is, there your heart will be also" (Matthew 6:19-21).

APPENDIX A

Letters between Jefferson and Danbury Baptist Association

The address of the Danbury Baptists Association in the state of Connecticut, assembled October 7, 1801.

To Thomas Jefferson, Esq., President of the United States of America.

Sir,

Among the many million in America and Europe who rejoice in your election to office; we embrace the first opportunity which we have enjoyed in our collective capacity, since your inauguration, to express our great satisfaction, in your appointment to the chief magistracy in the United States: And though our mode of expression may be less courtly and pompous than what many others clothe their addresses with, we beg you, sir, to believe that none are more sincere.

Our sentiments are uniformly on the side of religious liberty--that religion is at all times and places a matter between

God and individuals--that no man ought to suffer in name, person, or effects on account of his religious opinions--that the legitimate power of civil government extends no further than to punish the man who works ill to his neighbors; But, sir, our constitution of government is not specific. Our ancient charter together with the law made coincident therewith, were adopted as the basis of our government, at the time of our revolution; and such had been our laws and usages, and such still are; that religion is considered as the first object of legislation; and therefore what religious privileges we enjoy (as a minor part of the state) we enjoy as favors granted, and not as inalienable rights; and these favors we receive at the expense of such degrading acknowledgements as are inconsistent with the rights of freemen. It is not to be wondered at therefore; if those who seek after power and gain under the pretense of government and religion should reproach their fellow men-- should reproach their order magistrate, as a enemy of religion, law, and good order, because he will not, dare not, assume the prerogatives of Jehovah and make laws to govern the kingdom of Christ.

Sir, we are sensible that the president of the United States is not the national legislator, and also sensible that the national government cannot destroy the laws of each state; but our hopes are strong that the sentiments of our beloved president, which have had such genial effect already, like the radiant beams of the sun, will shine and prevail through all these states and all the world, till hierarchy and tyranny be destroyed from the earth. Sir, when we reflect on your past services, and see a glow of philanthropy and good will shining forth in a course of more than thirty years we have reason to believe that America's God has raised you up to fill the chair of state out of that goodwill which he bears to the millions which you preside over. May God strengthen you for your arduous task which providence and the voice of the people have called you-to sustain and support you and your administration against all the predetermined opposition of those who wish to raise to wealth and importance on the poverty and subjection of the people.

And may the Lord preserve you safe from every evil and bring you at last to his heavenly kingdom through Jesus Christ our Glorious Mediator.

Signed in behalf of the association,

Nehemiah Dodge
Ephraim Robbins
Stephen S. Nelson

Thomas Jefferson's Letter to the Danbury Baptist Association

To messers. Nehemiah Dodge, Ephraim Robbins, & Stephen S. Nelson, a committee of the Danbury Baptist association in the state of Connecticut.

Gentlemen

The affectionate sentiments of esteem and approbation which you are so good as to express towards me, on behalf of the Danbury Baptist association, give me the highest satisfaction. My duties dictate a faithful and zealous pursuit of the interests of my constituents, & in proportion as they are persuaded of my fidelity to those duties, the discharge of them becomes more and more pleasing.

Believing with you that religion is a matter which lies solely between Man & his God, that he owes account to none other for his faith or his worship, that the legitimate powers of government reach actions only, & not opinions, I contemplate with sovereign reverence that act of the whole American people which declared that their legislature should "make no law respecting an establishment of religion, or prohibiting the free exercise thereof," thus building a wall of separation between Church & State. Adhering to this expression of the supreme will of the nation in behalf of the rights of conscience, I shall see with sincere satisfaction the progress of those sentiments which tend to restore to man all his natural rights, convinced he has no natural right in opposition to his social duties.

I reciprocate your kind prayers for the protection & blessing of the common father and creator of man, and tender you for yourselves & your religious association, assurances of my high respect & esteem.

Th Jefferson
Jan. 1. 1802[1]

---

1. Bill of Rights Institute n.d.

APPENDIX B

Fetal Development

Weeks 1-3	Weeks 4-7
Day 1: fertilization: all human chromosomes are present; unique human life begins	**Week 4:** BY the end of week four the child is ten thousand times larger than the fertilized egg.
Day 6: embryo begins implantation in the uterus.	**Week 5:** Eyes, lets, and hands begin to develop.
Day 22: heart begins to beat with the child's own blood, often a different type than the mothers.	**Week 6:** Brain waves are detectable; mouth and lips are present; fingernails are forming.
Week 3: By the end of third week the child's backbone spinal column and nervous system are forming. The liver, kidneys, and intestines begin to take shape.	**Week 7:** Eyelids and toes form, nose distinct. The baby is kicking and swimming.

Weeks 8-10	Weeks 11-12
Week 8: Every organ is in place, bones begin to replace cartilage, and fingerprints begin to form. By the 8th week the baby can begin to hear. **Week 9 and 10:** Teeth begin to form, fingernails develop. The baby can turn his head, and frown. The baby can hiccup. The baby can "breathe" amniotic fluid and urinate between weeks 10 and 11.	**Week 11:** The baby can grasp objects placed in its hand; all organ systems are functioning. The baby has a skeletal structure, nerves, and circulation. **Week 12:** The baby has all of the parts necessary to experience pain, including nerves, spinal cord, and thalamus. Vocal cords are complete. The baby can suck its thumb.

Weeks 14-16	Weeks 17-20
Week 14: At this age, the heart pumps several quarts of blood through the body every day. **Week 15:** The baby has an adult's taste buds. **Week 16:** Bone marrow is now beginnings to form. The heart is pumping 25 quarts of blood a day. By the end of month 4 the baby will be 8-10 inches in length and will weigh up to half a pound.	**Week 17:** The baby can have dream (REM) sleep. **Week 19:** Babies can routinely be saved at 21 to 22 weeks after fertilization, and sometimes they can be saved even younger. **Week 20:** The earliest state at which partial birth abortions are performed. At 20 weeks the baby recognizes its' mothers voice.

Months 5-6	Months 7-9
Months 5 and 6: The baby practices breathing by inhaling amniotic fluid into it's developing lungs. The baby will grasp at the umbilical cord when it feels it. Most mothers feel an increase in movement, kicking, and hiccups from the baby. Oil and sweat glands are now functioning. The baby is now twelve inches long or more, and weighs up to one and a half pounds.	**Months 7-9:** Eyeteeth are present. The baby opens and closes his eyes. The baby is using four of the five senses (vision, hearing, taste, and touch). He knows the difference between waking and sleeping, and can relate to the moods of the mother. The baby's skin begins to thicken, and a layer of fat is produced and stored beneath the skin. Antibodies are built up, and the baby's heart begins to pump 300 gallons of blood per day. Approximately one week before birth the baby stops growing, and "drops" usually head down into the pelvic cavity.

This information was taken from the SEP Medical Clinic website that is located in Huntington Park, California.

http://sepmedical.com/first-trimester/

APPENDIX C

Washington Thanksgiving Day Proclamation

By the President of the United States of America. a Proclamation.

Whereas it is the duty of all Nations to acknowledge the providence of Almighty God, to obey his will, to be grateful for his benefits, and humbly to implore his protection and favor—and whereas both Houses of Congress have by their joint Committee requested me "to recommend to the People of the United States a day of public thanksgiving and prayer to be observed by acknowledging with grateful hearts the many signal favors of Almighty God especially by affording them an opportunity peaceably to establish a form of government for their safety and happiness."

Now therefore I do recommend and assign Thursday the 26th day of November next to be devoted by the People of these States to the service of that great and glorious Being, who is the beneficent Author of all the good that was, that is, or that will be—That we may then all unite in rendering unto him our sincere and humble thanks—for his kind care and protection of the People of this Country previous to their becoming a Nation—for the signal and manifold mercies, and the favorable interpositions of his Providence which we experienced in the course and conclusion of the late war—for the great degree of tranquillity, union, and plenty, which we have since enjoyed— for the peaceable and rational manner, in which we have been enabled to establish constitutions of government for our safety and happiness, and particularly the national One now lately instituted—for the civil and religious liberty with which we are blessed; and the means we have of acquiring and diffusing useful knowledge; and in general for all the great and various favors which he hath been pleased to confer upon us.

And also that we may then unite in most humbly offering our prayers and supplications to the great Lord and Ruler of Nations and beseech him to pardon our national and other transgressions—to enable us all, whether in public or private stations, to perform our several and relative duties properly and punctually—to render our national government a blessing to all the people, by constantly being a Government of wise, just, and constitutional laws, discreetly and faithfully executed and obeyed—to protect and guide all Sovereigns and Nations (especially such as have shewn kindness unto us) and to bless them with good government, peace, and concord—To promote the knowledge and practice of true religion and virtue, and the encrease of science among them and us—and generally to grant unto all Mankind such a degree of temporal prosperity as he alone knows to be best.

Given under my hand at the City of New-York the third day of October in the year of our Lord 1789.

Go: Washington[1]

---

1. Thanksgiving Proclamation, 3 October 1789 n.d.

APPENDIX D

Ronald Reagan Remarks at the Annual National Prayer Breakfast

Thank you, Mark, and thank all of you ladies and gentlemen. Before I say what I was planning to say this morning, Senator Javits, you concluded your readings with a prayer, and so, of course, I know, understood that we are—all of us—accustomed not to applauding prayer. But I can't help but think that all of us here have a hunger within us to applaud you for your presence here and what you have meant to this gathering.

And, Barbara, I had a terrible fear there for a few moments that you were going to make anything I had to say redundant. [Laughter] But I think that maybe the two fit together.

We all in this room, I know, and we know many millions more everywhere, turn to God in prayer, believe in the power and the spirit of prayer. And yet so often, we direct our prayers to those problems that are immediate to us, knowing that He has promised His help to us when we turn to Him. And yet in a world today that is so torn with strife where the divisions seem to be increasing, not people coming together, within countries, divisions within the people, themselves and all, I wonder if we have ever thought about the greatest tool that we have—that power of prayer and God's help.

If you could add together the power of prayer of the people just in this room, what would be its megatonnage? And have we maybe been neglecting this and not thinking in terms of a broader basis in which we pray to be forgiven for the animus we feel towards someone in perhaps a legitimate dispute, and at the same time recognize that while the dispute will go on, we have to realize that that other individual is a child of God even as we are and is beloved by God, as we like to feel that we are.

This power of prayer can be illustrated by a story that goes back to the fourth century. The Asian monk living in a little remote village, spending most of his time in prayer or tending the garden from which he obtained his sustenance—I hesitate to say the name because I'm not sure I know the pronunciation, but let me take a chance. It was Telemacmus, back in the fourth century. And then one day, he thought he heard the voice of God telling him to go to Rome. And believing that he had heard, he set out. And weeks and weeks later, he arrived there, having traveled most of the way on foot.

And it was at a time of a festival in Rome. They were celebrating a triumph over the Goths. And he followed a crowd into the Colosseum, and then there in the midst of this great crowd, he saw the gladiators come forth, stand before the Emperor, and say, "We who are about to die salute you." And he realized they were going to fight to the death for the entertainment of the crowds. And he cried out, "In the name of Christ, stop!" And his voice was lost in the tumult there in the great Colosseum.

And as the games began, he made his way down through the crowd and climbed over the wall and dropped to the floor of the arena. Suddenly the crowds saw this scrawny little figure making his way out to the gladiators and saying, over and over again, "In the name of Christ, stop." And they thought it was part of the entertainment, and at first they were amused. But then, when they realized it wasn't, they grew belligerent and angry. And as he was pleading with the gladiators, "In the name of Christ, stop," one of them plunged his sword into his body. And as he fell to the sand of the arena in death, his last words were, "In the name of Christ, stop."

And suddenly, a strange thing happened. The gladiators stood looking at this tiny form lying in the sand. A silence fell over the Colosseum. And then, someplace up in the upper tiers, an individual made his way to an exit and left, and others began to follow. And in the dead silence, everyone left the Colosseum. That was the last battle to the death between gladiators in the Roman Colosseum. Never again did anyone kill or did men kill each other for the entertainment of the crowd.

One tiny voice that could hardly be heard above the tumult. "In the name of Christ, stop." It is something we could be saying to each other throughout the world today.

Now, several days ago while I was very concerned about what I was going to say here today and trying to think of something to say, I received through diplomatic channels a message from far out across the Pacific. Sometime ago, our Ambassador presented to General Romulo of the Philippines the American Medal of Freedom. Not only had he been a great friend of the United States in our time of war, but then he had spent 17 years as an Ambassador here in Washington, from his country to ours. And for whatever reason, he sent this message of thanks to me for the medal that had been given, and then included the farewell statement that he had made when he left Washington, left this country, after those 17 years.

And I had to confess, I had never been aware that there had been such a farewell message, and I'm quite sure that many of you hadn't. And so, I'm going to share it with you. I think it fits what we're talking about today. He said, "I am going home,

America. For 17 years, I have enjoyed your hospitality, visited every one of your 50 States. I can say I know you well. I admire and love America. It is my second home. What I have to say now in parting is both tribute and warning.

"Never forget, Americans, that yours is a spiritual country. Yes, I know you're a practical people. Like others, I've marveled at your factories, your skyscrapers, and your arsenals. But underlying everything else is the fact that America began as a God-loving, God-fearing, God-worshiping people, knowing that there is a spark of the divine in each one of us. It is this respect for the dignity of the human spirit which keeps America invincible.

"May you always endure and, as I say again in parting, thank you, America, and farewell. May God keep you always, and may you always keep God."

Thank you.[1]

---

1.   The American Presidency Project n.d.

WORKS CITED

n.d. "18 U.S. Code § 1111." Accessed August 14, 2017. https://www.law.cornell.edu/uscode/text/18/1111.

2018. Abort 73. Janurary 22. http://abort73.com/abortion_facts/us_abortion_statistics/.

Andrews, Andy. 2011. How Do You Kill 11 Million People. Nashville, Tennessee: Thomas Nelson, Inc. .

Barber, James David. 1992. The Pulse of Politics: Electing Presidents in the Media Age. Transaction Publishers.

Barton, David. 1992. The Myth of Separation. Aledo, Texas: Wallbuilders Press.

n.d. Bill of Rights Institute. Accessed August 29, 2018. https://billofrightsinstitute.org/founding-documents/primary-source-documents/danburybaptists/.

Congress, 108th. 2004. "UNBORN VICTIMS OF VIOLENCE ACT." Accessed August 14, 2017. https://www.congress.

gov/108/plaws/publ212/PLAW-108publ212.pdf.

Dave Miller, Ph. D. 2017. God and Government. Montgomery: Apologetics Press.

—. 2014. Male and Female Roles: Gender in the Bible. Accessed August 26, 2018. http://apologeticspress.org/APContent.aspx?category=7&article=5007.

Engel v. Vitale. 1962. 370 U.S. 421 (Warren, June 25).

Griswold v. Connecticut. 1965. 381 U.S. 479 (Warren, June 7).
n.d. Guttmacher Institute. Accessed December 14, 2017. https://www.guttmacher.org/fact-sheet/induced-abortion-united-states.

Kaluger, George, and Meriem Fair Kaluger. 1979. Human Development: The Span of Life: Second Edition. St. Louis: The C.V. Mosby Co.

Kessler, Glenn. 2013. The Washington Post. June 13. Accessed December 14, 2017. https://www.washingtonpost.com/blogs/fact-checker/post/the-claim-that-the-incidence-of-rape-resulting-in-pregnancy-is-very-low/2013/06/12/936bc45e-d3ad-11e2-8cbe-1bcbee06f8f8_blog.html?noredirect=on&utm_term=.1192cab2c54b.

Lewis, C.S. 1944. The Abolition of Man. New York: Harper Collins.

Melisa M. Holmes, MD, Heidi S. Resnick, PhD, Dean G. Kilpatrick, PhD, Connie L. Best, PhD. 1996. Accessed December

14, 2017. https://www.ncbi.nlm.nih.gov/m/pubmed/8765248/.

Moore, Keith L., and T.V.N. Persaud. 2003. The Developing Human: Clinically Oriented Embryology (7th Edition). Philadelphia, Pennsylvania: Saunders.

Moore, Kieth L., and T.V.N. Persaud. 1993. The Devloping Human: Clinically Oriented Embryology 5th Edition. Philidelphia, Pennsylvania: Saunders.

Obergefell v. Hodges. 2015. 576 U.S. ___ (Roberts, June 26).

Reagan, Ronald. 1987. Ronald Reagan Foundation. June 12. Accessed September 25, 2017. https://www.reaganfoundation.org/media/51328/berlin.pdf.

Robinson, B.A. 2007. Religious Tolerance. Accessed August 14, 2017. http://www.religioustolerance.org/abo_whenl.htm.

Roe v. Wade. 1973. 410 U.S. 113 (Burger, Janurary 22).

Roseanne F. Zhao, Ph.D. 2014. The Y chromosome: beyond gender determination. May 30. Accessed August 29, 2018. https://www.genome.gov/27557513/the-y-chromosome-beyond-gender-determination/.

n.d. SEP Medical Clinic. Accessed Ocotber 13, 2017. http://sepmedical.com/first-trimester/.

Skousen, W. Cleon. 1981. The 5,000 Year Leap. Malta: National Center for Constitutional Studies.

THE POLITICAL CONSCIENCE OF THE CHRISTIAN

bib n.d. Statista. Accessed December 14, 2017. https://www.statista.com/statistics/191137/reported-forcible-rape-cases-in-the-usa-since-1990/#0.

n.d. Thanksgiving Proclamation, 3 October 1789. Accessed August 26, 2018. https://founders.archives.gov/documents/Washington/05-04-02-0091.

n.d. The American Presidency Project. Accessed August 26, 2018. http://www.presidency.ucsb.edu/ws/?pid=39211.

2009. "The Church's Role in the World." In The American Patriot's Bible, 1333. Richard G. Lee.

n.d. The James Madison Research Library and Information Center. Accessed August 27, 2018. http://www.madisonbrigade.com/library_bor.htm.

Webster, Noah. 1832. History of the United States. New Haven, Connecticut: Durrie & Peck.

62019390R00059

Made in the USA
Columbia, SC
01 July 2019